WITHDRAWN
UST
Libraries

THE IRISH COLLEGE AT LISBON

THE IRISH COLLEGE
AT LISBON
1590–1834

Patricia O Connell

FOUR COURTS PRESS

Set in 11 pt on 13.5 pt AGaramond by
Carrigboy Typesetting Services, County Cork for
FOUR COURTS PRESS LTD
Fumbally Court, Fumbally Lane, Dublin 8, Ireland
e-mail: info@four-courts-press.ie
http://www.four-courts-press.ie
and in North America for
FOUR COURTS PRESS
c/o ISBS, 5824 N.E. Hassalo Street, Portland, OR 97213.

© Patricia O Connell 2001

ISBN 1–85182–564–9

All rights reserved. No part of this publication may be
reproduced, stored in or introduced into a retrieval system,
or transmitted, in any form or by any means (electronic, mechanical,
photocopying, recording or otherwise), without the prior
written permission of both the copyright owner and
publisher of this book.

Printed in England
by MPG Books, Bodmin, Cornwall

To Maura, Annette, John and Nicholas
for their help and interest,
and to my late, lamented brother-in-law,
Garry Redmond, barrister, editor, raconteur,
who was second-to-none in his mastery of the English language

Preface

Some time before Lisbon's worst disaster, the earthquake of 1755, a senior official of the Patriarcado, the headquarters of the episcopal see of Lisbon, borrowed from the diocesan archives some documents relating to the history of the Patriarcado since its foundation in 1716. When the earthquake struck the city on All Saints Day, 1 November 1755, it was quickly followed by fires which destroyed what the quake had not obliterated, including material in the diocesan archives. The papers which were in the possession of the official survived and are now stored in the Biblioteca Nacional, Lisbon, among a collection of miscellaneous manuscripts of the Pombaline era.

This happening emphasizes the vulnerability of archival material and brings home to us that much of what we depend on for the history of the past may, in many cases, be hanging from a thread. We in Ireland know this from our own sad experience, since a large section of the records of our past was lost when the Four Courts was burned down in 1922 and the contents of the Public Records Office went up in flames. There are countless stories from all over the world of the loss of priceless documentary material, 'casualties' of wars and civil disasters.

In writing a study of the Irish College of St Patrick at Lisbon I was acutely aware of how dependent one is on the availability of records in libraries and archives throughout Europe and how exposed these are to the effects of war and strife and natural disasters of all kinds. This, of course, is in addition to the inroads of time and inadequate care over centuries into the fragile, flimsy life of documentary material – the faded ink, the tattered edges (which always seem to include an important date or even an essential word), the appetites of mites or worms and the discoloration of time.

The preceding musings are by way of explanation of the fragmentary character of this history of the Irish College, Lisbon. It is also a tribute to those sources of information which have made it possible to write the story at all: the marvellous collection of manuscript material, as yet uncodified, which I was privileged to be allowed to inspect at the Irish Jesuit Archives, through the good offices of the director, Dr Fergus O'Donoghue SJ, and the untiring and expert help of the archivist, Orna Sommerville; the collection of material brought back from Lisbon by the Dominican Fathers to the archives at St Mary's Priory, in Tallaght, relating to the Irish College, Lisbon, made available to me through the kindness and friendship of the archivist and historian, Father Hugh Fenning OP, and last, but by no means least, the interesting and valuable collection of letters and documents put at my disposal by the archivist, Mr David Sheehy, at the Dublin Diocesan Archives.

I also wish to record my deep gratitude to all the librarians and other archivists in Dublin, Maynooth, Galway and Lisbon, who have been so generous with their time and advice, among them Peter Folan, Librarian, Library of Mater Dei, Dublin, and his staff; Penny Woods, Russell Library, NUI Maynooth; Bernie Finan, James Hardiman Library, NUI Galway; the staff of the National Library of Ireland, as well as others too numerous to name. I would also like to express my thanks and appreciation to His Excellency John Campbell, Ambassador of Ireland to Portugal and to Michael Sanfey, First Secretary of the Irish Embassy in Lisbon for their unstinted help and support; to His Excellency D. Manuel Lopes da Costa, the former Ambassador of Portugal in Ireland and to His Excellency, D. João de Vallera, the present envoy of Portugal in Ireland for their generous interest and enthusiastic support of my work; to Rosario Hayes-McCoy, of the Portuguese Embassy for her valued friendship, shown to me in so many ways over the years and to Angela Delaforce, art historian and friend, for her guidance in Lisbon's archives and libraries and for her reading of the text of this work. My thanks are also due to the School of Irish Studies Foundation for an award for research on this book, to the Royal Irish Academy for the award of an Eoin O'Mahony Bursary in Irish History for the same purpose, and to the National University of Ireland for an award of grant in aid of publication of this volume. I am most appreciative of these three generous grants.

Lastly, I have much unfinished business in Portugal. I am deeply interested in investigating archives outside Lisbon, particularly in Évora, where the Irish connection was strong and where, I suspect, there is an interesting story to be found.

Contents

PREFACE		7
LIST OF ABBREVIATIONS		11
GLOSSARY OF PORTUGUESE WORDS		12
1	Introduction	13
2	Foundation and History	22
3	The Administration of the College	37
4	The Bishops	50
5	The Students	55
6	The Earthquake of 1755, and Other Troubles	100
7	The Last Years	115
8	Conclusion	130
BIBLIOGRAPHY		141
INDEX		143

Abbreviations

Bib. Nac. Lisboa	*Biblioteca Nacional, Lisboa*
ANTT	*Arquivo Nacional do Torre de Tombo*
Arch. Hib.	*Archivium Hibernicum*
AR	Annual Report
Coll. Hib.,	*Collectanea Hibernica*
DDA	Dublin Diocesan Archives
Fenning, 1	H. Fenning OP, 'Irishmen ordained at Lisbon, 1587–1625; 1641–60; 1669–1739; 1740–1850,' *Coll. Hib.* 31 and 32 (1989–90) 103–17.
Fenning, 2	Idem, *Coll. Hib.* 34 and 35 (1992–3) 59–76.
Fenning, 3	Idem, *Coll. Hib.* 36 and 37 (1994–6) 140–58.
G. da C.,	Manuel Gonçalves da Costa
LIS	Papers of the Irish College, Lisbon, Irish Jesuit Archives, Dublin
IDA	Irish Dominican Archives
IER	*Irish Ecclesiastical Record*
Knights	M.K. Walsh, *Spanish Knights of Irish Origin*
Meath List	Index to the Parish of Meath Diocese 1704–1993 (see Bibliography)
MT	MacErlean Transcripts, Irish Jesuit Archives, Dublin
NUI	National University of Ireland
RIA	Royal Irish Academy
Sal. Arch.,	*Salamanca Archives, NUI, Maynooth.*
Sea. AM	*Seanchas Ard Mhaca*

Glossary of Portuguese Words

bemfeitores	benefactors
convictores	boarders
feitorias	trading-post
fidalgo	nobleman
Marranos	crypto-Jews
mesa	board
ordinárias	fixed interest rates
quinta	country estate
retábulo	altar-piece

FOOTNOTES

To keep footnotes to a minimum I have frequently used one footnote to include several sources, which relate to the text immediately preceding the footnote number. I have tried to keep the sources in sequence as far as possible. The original spelling has been retained in quotations, etc.

CHAPTER 1

Introduction

Irish priests, monks, missionaries, pilgrims and scholars were not unknown on the European mainland, where they had always travelled, lived, worked and studied since Christianity came to Ireland in the fifth century. There is a general awareness of their contribution to the spread of Christianity and learning across the length and breadth of Europe, from Iceland to the mouth of the Danube, from Taranto to the Faroes. The list of saints and scholars is impressive: Colmcille, Columbanus, Brendan, Kilian, Fiachra, Fursey, Donatus, Cathaldus, Gaul, Colman, Virgilius of Salzburg and John Eriugena Scotus and many more, known not alone for their great piety but also for their wisdom, erudition and skill as preachers and missionaries. The Irish scholars and monks are justly credited with the preservation of much of Europe's heritage in their monasteries and libraries during the Dark Ages.

Several centuries later, however, when the religious revolution, termed 'The Reformation' raged throughout the continent a different kind of exile, no longer a voluntary one, was forced to leave Ireland and seek refuge on the mainland of Europe. This time the exiles were refugees, dispossessed Irish nobles, their families, their followers, soldiers, swordsmen, scholars and others, who were fleeing from savage and cruel treatment in their own country and arrived in continental ports with large numbers of expelled and persecuted bishops, priests, monks and, to a lesser degree and particularly in Cromwell's time, nuns.

In Ireland, from the time of Henry VIII's suppression and confiscation of the monasteries and his eventual break with Rome and the later enforcement of the Act of Supremacy by his daughter, Elizabeth I, there was a campaign of imprisonment and worse for those not prepared to acknowledge Henry or his daughter as supreme head of the church in their domains.

The confiscation of property, prohibition of Catholic education and many other disabilities were also inflicted on adherents to the old faith. Penal laws against Catholics were reinforced particularly after the reign of James II and it was not until to a limited degree only from the end of the eighteenth century, 1829, with Catholic Emancipation, that most of them were set aside.

Irish colleges or seminaries came into existence in many European countries from the late sixteenth century for a variety of reasons. They were primarily a consequence of the conversion of the English monarchs and their subjects to Protestantism, and the enforcement in Ireland of harsh laws aimed at the extirpation of the Catholic religion, to which the majority of the Irish had remained faithful.

Another reason was, without doubt, the difficulty of implementing the important recommendation of the Council of Trent (1545–63), as part of the Counter-Reformation, that seminaries should be set up for the training and education of aspirants to the priesthood.

It is not surprising that a papal bull, *Dum exquisita*, issued in 1564 by Pius IV, was highly critical of the state of education for the priesthood in Ireland. Catholics in general, whether clergy or laypeople, were barred from receiving a Catholic education and from various professions, including teaching. The lack of educational facilities for the training and education of clergy, the impossibility of setting up such facilities and the confiscations of monasteries and clerical schools combined to make the setting up of seminaries outside Ireland imperative; the papal bull of 1564 has rightly been described as 'a blueprint for the Irish continental colleges'.[1] The church authorities resolved on this course of action, even though it was against the law for students to go abroad to study. Those who did so would be liable to rigorous penalties, if caught on their return.

The Portuguese were acutely aware of the special position of Ireland in what was called 'Protestant Northern Europe.' A report to the provincial of the Jesuits in Portugal in 1605 points out that the Irish sent their sons to universities in the Catholic kingdoms of Europe to study the humanities and sacred theology so that, well-instructed in the Catholic faith, they would return to their country to refute the errors of the heretics.[2]

Twenty-nine Irish colleges came into existence in a number of European countries between 1578 and 1680. Twelve were founded by the major religious orders such as Franciscans, Dominicans, Augustinians, Capuchins and Carmelites.[3] The remaining seventeen were exclusively for the

---

[1] T.J. Walsh, *The Irish continental college movement* (Dublin, 1973), p. 34.
[2] Manuel Gonçalves da Costa (hereinafter G. da C.), *Fontes inéditas portuguesas para a história de Irlanda* (Braga, 1981), p. 234. [3] The Franciscans had colleges in Louvain, Prague, Vielan, Capranica and Rome; the Dominicans in Lisbon, Louvain and Rome (San Clemente); the Augustinians in Rome (San Matteo Merulana); the Capuchins in Charleville; the Carmelites in La Rochelle and Aix-

INTRODUCTION

education of secular or diocesan clergy.[4] My area of research interest is with this second category and primarily with the six in Spain and Portugal – Lisbon,[5] Salamanca, Santiago de Compostela, Seville, Madrid and Alcalá de Henares.

The colleges for secular clergy in the Iberian peninsula were, in general, governed by Jesuits, but although some of the clerics trained in them later entered the Society of Jesus, the majority returned to Ireland as secular priests. In the Spanish Netherlands colleges were set up in Douai, Antwerp, Lille, Tournai and Louvain. The Irish College in Rome was founded in 1628.

In 1578 Father John Lee, of the diocese of Meath, established, in Paris, the first Irish College for diocesan clergy on the continent. Other colleges followed in Bordeaux, Rouen, Toulouse and Nantes. Father Lee had left Ireland with six clerical students, to enrol at the College de Montaigu, a college of the University of Paris. The group formed a society known as the Community of Irish Students in Paris. Later they were taken under the protection of the president of the Parliament of Paris, the Baron de St-Just, Jean de l'Escalopier, who, in 1605, bought a house for them and maintained them from his own funds.[6] They moved to other houses as their numbers grew. The present college still functions, not as a seminary, but as a centre for Irish students, scholars and visitors to the French capital. It is in a prime location, near the Sorbonne and the Pantheon, and has for many years opened its doors to researchers and to others, who wish to stay there. The present building was bought in 1769, on a street called the 'rue du Cheval Vert' – but its name has since been changed to 'rue des irlandais'.[7]

Most of the Irish seminaries in France were closed and confiscated by 1793, four years after the Revolution began. In Spain the colleges run by the Jesuits had already been closed and confiscated in 1769, when the Society was suppressed in that kingdom. St Patrick's College in Lisbon was confiscated ten years earlier during the regime of the notoriously anticlerical Marquês de Pombal.

Some years after the foundation of the Irish College in Paris – about 1590 – the Clonmel Jesuit, Thomas White, tried to set up a similar college

---

la-Chapelle. See also T.J. Walsh, op. cit., pp 36–87. **4** Of the seventeen colleges for secular priests five were in Spain, one in Portugal, five in France, five in the Low Countries and one in Italy. **5** Portugal was under Spanish rule for 58 years (1582–1640), during which time the Irish College of St Patrick was set up in Lisbon (1590–1834). **6** J. O'Boyle, *The Irish colleges on the continent: their origin and history* (Belfast, 1935), pp 31–2. **7** See L. Swords, *Soldiers, scholars, priests* (Paris, 1985). An ambitious scheme is in the pipeline for the restoration and

in Valladolid.[8] He himself had been a student at the University of Valladolid, where there were many Irish refugee clerical students. He brought them together in a small college, which he maintained during its short life from his own pocket. A document dated 1608 affirms, that

> Father Thomas White ... seeing so manie poor scholars of his nation in great miserie at Valladolid, having no means to continue their studie, nor language to begge, having given overhis private commoditie, did recollect and reduce them to oneplace, which he maintained by his industrie and begging, until, by his petition to Philip the Second, in the year, 1593, a College of Irish students was founded.[9]

In 1592, having been successful in getting royal sanction for the funding of a college for aspirants to the diocesan priesthood, Father White abandoned his fledgling seminary in Valladolid and brought the nine students from it to the beautiful golden city on the Tormes river to the new foundation at Salamanca, the Royal College of St Patrick for Irish Nobles, 'el real colegio de San Patrício de nobles irlandeses'.[10] This college became in time the flagship of the Irish College network.

Undoubtedly, the majority of the secular or diocesan priests, and, indeed, many bishops, trained on the continent for the Irish mission, came from the larger Irish Colleges at Paris, Rome or Salamanca. However, the smaller colleges also sent many clerics to the hard-pressed Irish Church

development of this outstanding Irish centre in the French capital. **8** Valladolid, in the central meseta of Castile, was an important centre, the seat of an archbishopric with a venerable university, and had been the principal residence of the kings of Castile until Philip II moved his capital to Madrid in 1560. An English college was founded there in 1589 by the English Jesuit, Robert Persons (1596–1610), and a Scottish college was transferred there from Madrid in 1771. Even though no college was set up formally there, it is important, I think, to remember Irish associations with Valladolid because of the many Irish exiles – for example, Father Thomas White and others – who lived there. **9** E. Hogan SJ, *Distinguished Irishmen of the sixteenth century* (London, 1894), p. 49, quoted from John Coppinger's *Mnemosymum to the Catholics in Ireland (1608)*, p. 268. **10** The title may be explained by the fact that many of the early candidates for the priesthood would have come from the ranks of the Irish and Old English nobility. The college was affiliated to the University of Salamanca, which was, with the universities of Paris, Bologna and Oxford, one of the four most important at that time in Europe. It dated from 1218, and had c.10,000 students and twenty-five

INTRODUCTION

from the end of the sixteenth century, until their closure in the latter half of the eighteenth century. All of the colleges in the Iberian peninsula, except Alcalá de Henares, were run by the Jesuits, and over the years there were exchanges and co-operation among them. In time, Santiago came to be a centre for the study of philosophy, and the collegians after a two-year course there went on to the Irish College in Salamanca, where they completed their studies in theology and were ordained.[11] The whole course of study lasted seven years and lectures were given in Latin. Therefore, it was imperative, that the students should be well-versed in Latin on arrival in Spain or Portugal. This was somewhat difficult for students coming from Ireland, in view of the religious persecution there in the seventeenth and eighteenth centuries.[12]

Normally the students entered the seminary at about eighteen years of age. On the completion of their course, if they wanted to return to Ireland as fully-trained priests, the seminarists made application to the king for a 'viaticum'. This was a sum of one hundred ducats[13] given to each returning priest to cover the cost of his journey home and, in addition, to enable him to buy secular clothing, since it was prohibited not only to leave Ireland for an education but also to return there as a priest.[14] In 1709, for example, the rector of the

---

colleges in the sixteenth century. **11** In some cases, because of the shortage of priests in Ireland, clerics were ordained before receiving their full education on condition that they enrol, at a later date, in one of the continental seminaries. **12** Latin and Greek were taught in underground schools all over Ireland. Some names of teachers are given in the 'oaths', taken by the students, when they enrolled in the colleges; in these they promised to abide by the rules of the college and to return to Ireland, when their studies were completed. **13** The ducat, *ducado*, was a gold coin worth 11 *reales* plus 1 *maravedí* (a copper coin of low value) or 375 *maravedís*; 1 *real*, a silver coin, was worth 34 *maravedís*; 1 *escudo* was worth 10 *reales*. A captain's pay at that time was roughly 40 ducats a month. In Portugal the sum was paid to the returning cleric in *milreis*. The *real* (plural, *reis*) was abolished in the sixteenth century, but its multiples, such as *milreis* (a thousand *reis*) were retained to use as money of accounts: see C.R. Boxer, *The Portuguese seaborne empire, 1415–1825* (Manchester, 1991), p. 391. See also D.J. O'Doherty 'Students of the Irish College Salamanca (1595–1619)', *Arch. Hib.* 2 (1913) 7. The subject of money, weights and measures, and their relation with payments in kind, in Spain from the sixteenth to the nineteenth centuries is complex and it is difficult to give equivalents in our modern terms. Nonetheless, comparisons are a useful criterion. Although St Teresa of Ávila belongs to an earlier period (1515–82), her income from a farm, left to her by her mother, is of interest. From the moment that she entered the convent she received each year an amount of 25 *fanegas* of wheat from her property. Many payments were made in kind, and the *fanega* was a measure of grain, more or less equal to a bushel and a half. **14** Laws to this

Salamanca college, requesting the *viaticum* for five priests recently ordained, said in his petition, 'They disguise themselves as sailors to escape discovery, when they leave the ship on arrival in Ireland.'[15] The usual route home was through the port of Bilbao. Generally, the young priest had to wait in the port for good weather, for the departure of a ship for Ireland and, most importantly, for a captain disposed to risk arrest on arrival in an Irish port. With all these uncertainties and the many days – sometimes, weeks – at sea and travel-time over land, the journey could take considerable time. There is the case of one student, who had been expelled in 1747 from Salamanca, having to spend two weeks in Lisbon before being able to embark for his return journey: Francis Bermingham, from the diocese of Tuam, left Salamanca under a cloud on 3 February 1747; he wrote two letters to the rector, John O'Brien (1743–60) during his protracted wait for a ship in Lisbon.[16]

Another letter to Father O'Brien, dated 16 November 1754[17] from Father John Michael White SJ, Dublin, a former student at the college, gives us a colourful account of the landing of a ship from Spain in Ardmore, County Waterford, some time before 1754. The story is not untypical. The ship made the journey in ten days, the voyage was uneventful except for a great storm one night which

> had like to split us on the rocks of Scilly, as the winds blew us strongly in on them ... About four in the morning the sky cleared up, and the sea and winds settled, so without further danger we proceeded by the side of England till we came into the Irish Channel. I landed in Ardmore, a small village between Youghal and Dungarvan, on account of some vagabond weavers, who were banished out of Spain. The ship was bound to Ross, whither they also went. I was kindly received and handed out of the boat by a Protestant Gentlewoman, who with numbers of people came to the shore surprised at the ship's long delay; and, talking, she told me afterwards, she knew very well what I was by my appearance. She entertained me splendidly for two days and sent

effect were enacted under James I. See O'Boyle, op. cit., pp 237–50. **15** *Sal. Arch.*, *legajo* 40/7, document in Spanish: 'Se disfrazan de marineros para escapar el descubrimiento cuando dejarán el buque al llegar a Irlanda.' **16** R.W. Richardson (ed.), *Salamanca letters* (Maynooth, 1995), p. 9, letters numbers 13 AA 1 74 and 75: '... my arrival in Lisbon after a dreary, tedious journey and such I did not think it would be. I wish I had come a horse back with all my heart ... we delayed fourteen days by land and then half-a-day by water ... there is a ship here bound for Dublin, but am not sure when she will depart.' **17** *Salamanca letters*, 13 AA 1 122.

INTRODUCTION

for the parish priest, Mr Power, who staid with her while I was there. She also furnished me with a house gratis.

He states that he saw Mr Lisward in Dungarvan and Mr St Leger and Mr Shea in Waterford and all of them were well. These three men were all Jesuits and former Salamanca students. He adds that he went from Waterford to Kilkenny and on to Dublin by stage-coach.[18]

The history of the exiled seminarians and of the Irish College movement in Europe is an inspiring human saga. After a long period of study abroad the newly-trained priests returned to a land, where life was harsh, difficult and sometimes dangerous. From 1590 to the end of the eighteenth century, by which time the laws against Catholics had been considerably relaxed, the Irish Church lived virtually underground.

In spite of its undoubted importance, surprisingly little has been published on the history of the Irish colleges on the continent. All of the colleges in Spain and Portugal were founded between 1590 and 1649. Most of them functioned until the end of the eighteenth century. The one exception is Salamanca, which survived until 1951; yet, even so, a comprehensive study of this most important last survivor has never been written.[19] The seminary of St Patrick in Lisbon (1590–1834) is scarcely mentioned in any of the accounts of the history of the Irish colleges on the continent of Europe. The present book tries to remedy this state of affairs, to redress the balance and offer a study of some aspects of this important Irish college. Nonetheless some excellent articles and monographs have appeared, on the subject of the Lisbon college, most of which have been listed, up to 1994, by Regina Whelan Richardson in her important bibliography in *The Maynooth Library Treasures*.[20]

The earliest available writings on the colleges include a series of anonymous articles in the sadly defunct *Irish Ecclesiastical Record*.[21] These

18 Edward Lisward SJ ministered in Ireland until he returned to Salamanca on 15 September 1761 to take over as rector of the Irish college there (1761–6). John St Leger SJ was also a former Salamanca man and worked with Father Shea SJ in the Waterford diocese.   **19** The neglect of the story of the Irish colleges on the continent is general, but even more remarkable is that of the colleges in Spain since the deposit, in Ireland, of the Salamanca Archives in 1950/1, and their accessibility in the Russell Library, National University of Ireland, Maynooth. This significant and valuable collection of papers includes records from almost all the colleges, with the exception of Lisbon.   **20** Ed. Agnes Neligan (RIA, Dublin 1995), pp 144–7.   **21** 'Irish colleges since the Reformation' *IER* 8, (1871), 307–13; 9 (1872), 1–5, 137–42.

were followed by another series in the same journal by William McDonald, rector of St Patrick's College, Salamanca in 1871–6. McDonald's articles are long and diffuse, full of information and interesting quotations, but short (or sometimes totally lacking) on precise details of provenance.[22]

Denis J. O'Doherty, another former rector of Salamanca, also contributed a very useful and detailed series of articles to *Archivium Hibernicum*, on students at the Irish College, Salamanca, from 1619 to 1796.[23] Francis Finegan, in a long line of eminent Jesuit historians, including John MacErlean,[24] has also contributed an important article on the Irish rectors at Seville from 1619 to 1687.[25] The writings of John J. Silke on the battle of Kinsale and its aftermath, on the students of the Irish College, Seville, and the Irish abroad from 1534 to 1691[26] are essential reading for all students of the sixteenth and seventeenth centuries in relation to Irish history. Also essential are the numerous publications of Professor Patrick Corish which manifest his professional insight and practised approach to the subject of the Irish continental colleges.[27]

The most notable contributions on the subject of the Lisbon college are those of Manuel Gonçalves da Costa and Hugh Fenning OP. Gonçalves da Costa's work is fundamental to any study of the links between Ireland and Portugal from the sixteenth century. He has put together detailed listings of sources for the history of the Irish College of St Patrick, in Lisbon, and of many other aspects of the period under study.[28]

---

22 W. McDonald, 'Irish Colleges since the Reformation', *IER* 8 (1871), 465–73; 'Irish ecclesiastical colleges since the Reformation' (Seville), *IER* 9 (1871) 208–21; 'Irish colleges since the Reformation' (Madrid, Alcalá), *IER* 9 (1872), pp 544–7; 'Irish ecclesiastical Colleges since the Reformation' (Santiago), *IER* 10 (1873), pp 167–81, 196–211, 245–59; 290–303; 'Irish ecclesiastical colleges since the Reformation' (Salamanca), *IER* 10 (1874), 353–66, 449–63, 519–32, 553–67, *IER* 11 (1874), 1–13, 101–40. **23** *Arch. Hib.* 2 (1913), 1–36: 3 (1914), 87–112; 4 (1915), 1–58. **24** The MacErlean Collection consists of transcripts made by John MacErlean, SJ (1870–1950), in a wide range of European archives, of documents of Irish Jesuit interest in particular and of Irish interest in general. The collection is of prime importance. The material is filed in chronological order from 1567 to 1735 in the Irish Jesuit Archives, Dublin, code MT. Another significant collection in the same archives, the Papers of the Irish College, Lisbon is filed under LIS/1–10. **25** 'The Irish rectors at Seville, 1619–87', *IER* 106 (July/December 1966), 5th series, 45–63. **26** *Kinsale: the Spanish intervention in Ireland at the end of the Elizabethan wars* (Liverpool, 1970, reprinted Dublin, 2000); 'The Irish College, Seville', *Arch. Hib.*, 24 (1961) 103–47; 'The Irish abroad, 1534–1691' in *New history of Ireland*, ed. Moody et al. (Oxford, 1976), iii, pp 587–633. **27** 'Correspondence of the Superiors of the Jesuit mission in Ireland and John O'Brien SJ, rector of Salamanca', *Arch. Hib.* 27 (1964) 85–103; *Catholic communities in the seventeenth and eighteenth centuries* (Dublin, 1981). **28** *Fontes inéditas*, op. cit.

INTRODUCTION

The difficult and onerous task of searching in the ordination registers of the *patriarcado* (the diocesan offices of the see of Lisbon) for Irish priests ordained in Lisbon, between 1587 and 1850, was completed and presented by Hugh Fenning in *Collectanea Hibernica*. This work is also basic to any investigation of the history of Irish clerics who studied and worked in Portugal during the relevant centuries. In his work he records the ordination details not only of Dominicans, but those of secular priests and of other religious orders in Lisbon for nearly three hundred years.[29]

Important contributions have been made by Spanish scholars including Amalio Huarte,[30] José Couselo Bouzas,[31] María–José Arnáiz/José Luís Sancho[32] and E. Rivera Vázquez[33] on aspects of the history of the Irish colleges in Spain. Some recent works on the Spanish colleges, in particular, have appeared since 1994, when the Bibliography mentioned above stopped.[34] In spite of the scholarly contributions to our knowledge of the Irish College network and its proud history over three centuries. the full story of the priests, trained in Spain or Portugal, has still to be told. Many gaps still exist in the coverage given to these colleges and in those in the Low Countries, Bohemia and Italy. The colleges in France have been better served.[35]

---

29 Fenning, 1, 2 and 3. loc. cit., xxxi and xxxii (1989–90), pp 103–17; xxxiv–xxxv 59–76 (1992–3); xxxvi–xxxvii (1994–6), pp 140–58. **30** 'Petitions of Irish students in the University of Salamanca, 1574–1591', *Arch. Hib.*, 4 (1915), 96–130. **31** *Estudios gallegos: El colegio de irlandeses de Santiago de Compostela* (Santiago, 1935). **32** *El colegio de los irlandeses* (Alcalá de Henares, 1985). **33** *Galicia y los jesuitas. Sus colegios y enseñanza en los siglos xvi al xvii* (Santiago, 1989), chapter xii. **34** Oscar Recio Morales, 'The Irish College at Alcalá de Henares in a Europeen perspective' (minor thesis, St Patrick's College, Maynooth, 1995); Patricia O Connell *Arch Hib.*, 'The Irish College, Santiago de Compostela: 1605–1767', *Arch Hib.* 50 (1996), 19–28; *idem*, 'The rectors and students of the Irish College at Alcalá de Henares, Spain, 1649–1785', *Seanchas Ard Mhacha* 8 (1996–7), 77–88; *idem*, *The Irish College at Alcalá de Henares, 1649–1785* (Dublin, 1997); Corrections: 'The Irish College at Alcalá de Henares', *Sea AM* 17 (1998) 165; Karin Schüller, *Die bezichungen zwischen Spanien und Irland im 16 und 17 Jahrhundert: diplomatie, handel und die soziale integration katholoscher exulanten* (Münster, 1999); Patricia O Connell, 'The early-modern Irish College network in Iberia, 1590–1800', in T. O'Connor (ed.), *The Irish in Europe, 1580–1815* (Dublin, 2001), pp 49–64. **35** See Liam Swords, op. cit., *The Irish French connection* (Paris, 1978); Thomas O'Connor, 'Thomas Messenger (*c.*1575–1638?) and the seventeenth-century Irish church', *Ríocht na Midhe* 11 (2000) 88–105; 'Some historiographical remarks' in T. O'Connor (ed.), op. cit., pp 9–26.

CHAPTER 2

Foundation and History

In one of the oldest and most beautiful quarters of the city of Lisbon there is a building, which has deep-rooted associations with Ireland. Number 7, Escadinhas de São Crispim, in the rua de São Mamede,[1] atop steep steps on a street which winds down to the river Tagus, is the building which formerly housed the Irish College of St Patrick ('O collégio da Santa Fé Catholica dos estudantes irlandeses sob a invocação de São Patrício'). Founded at the end of the sixteenth century as a seminary for the education of Irish secular priests and clerical students, the college was popularly called the 'house of the *Hibérnicos*'[2] and as the 'College of St Patrick'. After many vicissitudes – plague, earthquake, wars and closures, *exclaustração*[3] – the college, which was run for many years by the Jesuits, finally closed in 1834.

The history of the Irish College of St Patrick is inextricably linked with that of the Irish Dominican community and their church of Corpo Santo,[4]

---

1 Translation: 'the steps of St Crispin in St Mamede Street.' The college was within the parish of St Mamede until the parish boundaries were re-drawn in the eighteenth century. Wherever passages appear in Portuguese or other languages, translations are given hereafter in footnotes.   **2** See Baltasar Matos Caeiro, *Os conventos de Lisboa*, São Patrício (*Os Hibérnicos*) (Lisboa, 1989). I am indebted to my friend, Patricia Lambe, Lisbon, for this reference.   **3** *A exclaustração* was the suppression in 1759 of the Society of Jesus and the confiscation of its property in Portugal. This was during the regime of Sebastião José de Carvalho e Mello, marquis of Pombal (1699–1782), who virtually controlled the country until the death of King José in 1777, when he was dismissed.   **4** The Dominican house in Lisbon was founded in 1634 by Dominic O'Daly OP and was known as the 'Church and College of the Holy Rosary', later changed to 'Corpo Santo'. The origin of the names is linked to a shrine to São Telmo, St Elmo, a martyred bishop in Italy, the patron saint of mariners. The expression St Elmo's Fire was well-known to sailors. It was a light, seen at night at sea – a glow accompanying the slow discharge of electricity to earth from the atmosphere, which was called Corposanto in Italy. After the martyrdom of St Elmo, mariners believed that he sent this light to help and guide them. There was a shrine to this saint on the site where the Irish Dominican church was built – hence the name Corpo Santo. The church was destroyed in the earthquake of 1755, but was soon rebuilt. It became with the Irish Dominican sisters of the convent of Nossa Senhora de Bom Sucesso,[5] and with the lives of the many Irish, laymen and women, who lived and died there and who found refuge and homes in Portugal. Each is an integral part of the history of the Irish in Portugal in the seventeenth, eighteenth and nineteenth centuries, and also an important part of the social, ecclesiastical and political history of Ireland and of the Irish participation in the Counter-Reformation.

Spain was in the forefront of the Catholic Counter-Reformation; but, apart altogether from religious reasons, Spain was a first choice for many of the Irish emigrés because of the traditional links between Ireland and Spain in political, commercial and cultural spheres. The accessibility of the two countries to each other, and the long-established sea trade-routes, were also important factors. The king of Spain ruled Portugal from 1580 to 1640, and this union of the two countries under Philip II[6] and subsequent rulers helps explain why Irish exiles opted for Portugal. There had, of course, since medieval times been strong fishery and trade links between Lisbon and the Irish ports of Dublin, Waterford, Limerick and Galway.

The year of the foundation of the College of St Patrick is generally given as 1593, and the Irish Jesuit, John Howling, as its founder, aided by Pedro Fonseca, a wealthy and aristocratic Portuguese Jesuit, who was

---

the centre of Dominicans of the Irish province until the 1830s, when the Irish province was re-established after more than three hundred years, with the building of the Dominican house of studies (*studium generale*) in Tallaght, County Dublin. **5** The convent of Nossa Senhora do Bom Sucesso was founded, also, by Father Dominic O'Daly in 1639, with the help of Dona Iria de Brito, Condesa de Atalaya. The Irish Dominican sisters still run the convent, in Belém on the outskirts of Lisbon, as a school and are involved in many activities with various disadvantaged communities in the city. A booklet, *Convento de Bom Sucesso, 1639–1989*, was published by the convent on the occasion of the 350th anniversary of the foundation. **6** When King Henrique, the cardinal-king of Portugal, died in 1580, a serious dynastic crisis ensued. As the cardinal was childless, several claimants to the throne came forward. These included Philip II of Spain; Catarina, duchess of Braganza; António, prior of Crato; Philibert, duke of Savoy; and Ranuccio, duke of Parma. King Philip II of Spain inherited the throne in 1582. The period of Spanish rule is referred to as the '*dominio filipino*', when the kingdom was ruled by Philip II, III and IV of Spain. Philip II was supportive of the Irish cause throughout his reign. See José Hermano Saraiva, *Portugal: a companion history* (Manchester, 1997), p. 64.

undoubtedly one of its original benefactors.[7] There is documentary evidence, however, that the college was initially set up in 1590. In its 'Book of Foundation' it is categorically stated, that the seminary was instituted in that year, with twenty collegians, young Irishmen gathered together by Garcia de Melho de Silva, their founder and protector.[8] This version would mean that it was the first Irish college in the Iberian Peninsula – earlier than Salamanca, founded in 1592, which has hitherto been regarded as the earliest.

According to documents from the same source the first home of the fledgling Irish college was in the Jesuit foundation, São Roque.[9] Later, a house was rented by Father Fonseca in the Mouraria quarter of Lisbon, 'estava então em Nossa Senhora da Gloria, junto das casas do Conde de Castro'.[10] From there it moved for a while to a site near the chapel of Santa Ana; and after that to houses offered by the Conde de Castanheira, near the dwelling of the *regador* (governor), Manuel de Vasconcelos, in 'Nossa Senhora da Gloria que e una hermida que esta sobre as portas da Anunciada ... A hermida da Senhora da Gloria ja desapareceu, mas o local conserva o

---

7 O'Boyle, op. cit., p. 179; E. Hogan, op. cit., p. 42. Several names have been mentioned as founder: John Howling SJ, Pedro Fonseca SJ, Garcia de Melho da Sylva, Duarte da Costa SJ, and António Fernandes Ximenes. Father Howling was born in Wexford in 1542 and joined the Society of Jesus about 1573. It is recorded that he was in Alcalá de Henares in 1577 when his friend, Dr William Walsh, bishop of Meath (1554–77) and suffragan to the archbishop of Toledo, died. He was also present in Lisbon at the death-bed of Nicholas Skerret, archbishop of Tuam (1580–3). He wrote biographies of the Irish martyrs killed between 1578 and '88. See Hogan, pp 29–47. His friend, Pedro de Fonseca, was an eminent Jesuit philosopher and theologian. He was a generous friend of Ireland. See Hogan, p. 42. **8** LIS/3: ' ... consta ser fundado e instituido no anno de 1590 com 20 collegiais mancebos que nelle estanao recolhidos irlandeses, por Garcia de Melho da Sylva fundador, instituidor, e Protector delle em sua vida.' Translation: ' ... it was founded in the year 1590 with twenty youthful collegians, who were gathered in it by Garcia de Melho da Sylva, founder and protector of it for his lifetime'. He was regarded not alone as founder, but because he was a *fidalgo velho,* was given the title of protector and judge of the Irish students. See G. da C., p. 204; MT 22. Jan. 1593. The rules of the college were also dated 1590: G. da C., pp 201–2. **9** LIS/3: 'O seminario irlandes começoa na Casa de S Roque, ... no ano de 1590 fizera huma Irmandade de Min.ros reais e fidalgos pa comt ... esmolas o sustenarem ... ' Translation: The Irish seminary began in St Roque ... in the year 1590 a brotherhood was set up of royal ministers and nobles to provide alms to sustain it' (MT, 8 April 1593). **10** LIS/3. Translation: ' ... it was then beside Our Lady of Glory, near the houses of the Count of Castro.'

nome'.[11] This is not far from São Roque. In this house students were installed on 29 June 1590, thus giving the start to the College of St Patrick of Lisbon 'o primeiro que se fundou de Irlandeses na Christiandade'.[12] The foundation was a reward for the Irish, as King Philip II, apparently, 'had regard to the loyalty with which the Irish nation had always served the House of Austria', the Hapsburgs.[13]

Finding that this house did not satisfy the needs of the college, several moves were made, and its final domicile was, as I have said, on the Escadinhas de São Crispim on the elevated site in the old and picturesque quarter near the castle of St George and Sé (short for *Sedes Epistolis*) where the cathedral of the patriarch of Lisbon[14] stands. It is also close to the church of the patron saint of Lisbon and Portugal, St Anthony, a church much revered by the *lisboetas*.

In their first dwelling the collegians were maintained by *uma mesa*,[15] a board of benefactors, generally referred to as *fidalgos* or noblemen, funded by *esmolas* or alms, raised and contributed by the *fidalgos*, and, in part, by the Ministérios de Facenda and Justiça (Ministries of Finance and Justice). The institution was under royal protection in the reign of 'Dom Phelippe o prudente ... e governado em seu lugar o Cardeal Archduque Alberto, Viserei de Portugal.[16]

A IRMANDADE

The college was ruled, in fact, for fifteen years, 1590–1605, by the board of *fidalgos* and royal ministers, '*dos mais graves do Reino*'.[17] This group of

---

11 Ibid. Translation: '(The church of) Our Lady of Glory, which is a hermitage near the entrance to the (church of) the Annunciation ... the hermitage has disappeared but the locality keeps the name.' **12** Ibid. Translation: ' ... the first founded for the Irish in Christendom.'   **13** Ibid. 'Dom Phelipe (Philip II) avendo respeito a lealdade com que a nação irlandeza sempre servio a Casa de Austria'.
14 The title of patriarch was conferred on the archbishop of Lisbon in 1716.
15 The Misericórdia, or to give it its full title, the Santa Casa da Misericórdia, the major charitable lay-brotherhood in Lisbon, had a board of guardians called a *mesa*. The board of the Irmandade of the Irish college was on the same lines.
16 Translation: 'Philip the Prudent and governed in his name by the Cardinal Archduke Albert, Viceroy of Portugal.' Philip the Prudent was Philip II of Spain, and I of Portugal. The cardinal duke was his nephew, viceroy of Portugal.
17 Translation: ' ... the gravest in the kingdom': G. da C., p. 203.

benefactors was formed into a brotherhood or confraternity, a *irmandade*, and included some of the most important and influential personages of the time, representing some of the principal families at court. These people helped to sustain the college for many years with their annual financial contributions to its upkeep. The collegians themselves had to collect the alms for the upkeep of the infant establishment from both the patrons and entrance-door collections (*esmolas de portal*), until the situation was regularized by the institution of the *ordinárias*[18] in 1608.

There were also some Jesuits on the board – Fathers John Howling and Juan de Lucena and Pedro Fonseca, in 1593, and Fathers Nicholas Leynich, and Nuno Mascarenhas in 1600. Two laymen, Juan de Lasse (John de Lacy) and Tomás Geraldino (Thomas Fitzgerald), appear on the elected board in 1593.[19]

It was recommended that elections to the board of this brotherhood should be held every year or, at least, every two years, and that the members should also contribute the *esmolas* for the maintenance of the college. In fact, elections were held in 1593, '95, '96, '97, 1600 and 1605, apparently from a pool of members of the confraternity.[20] For example, some thirty of these benefactors were members of the first board in 1590 and included members of many eminent and important families, who were moved by the plight of the refugee seminarians and in their charity sought to help them.[21]

Garcia de Melho da Silva, the first chairman and judge of the *irmandade*, was the son of Diego de Melho and Caterina de Castro and was *fidalgo velho*, old nobility. He was also a member of the royal council. He died in 1600. John Howling apparently looked askance at the stewardship of the chairman. In a letter in 1592 to Thomas Strong, bishop of Ossory, he expresses the opinion that in external things, such as the garb of the collegians, de Melho da Silva was generous, but that in more essential matters there was great difficulty in gaining anything from him.[22]

18 The *ordinárias* were fixed-interest rates instituted by the crown: G. da C., 'St Patrick's School of Lisbon', p. 37.   **19** MT 1 Feb. 1593 and 4 April 1600.   **20** Ibid. 1593–1605 and LIS/3 (*Fundação* f.296/7).   **21** The names of members of the brotherhood are to be found also in MT 1593–1605.   **22** G. da C., *Fontes*, p. 209, letter dated 26 May 1592: 'Our students shall go in habits like students of the Seminary, but somewhat different in colour. In these external things (Senhor) Garsia is liberal, but for things of more necessity and substance there is great difficulty to get anything from him.' Walter French wrote in similar terms to Bishop Thomas Strong of Ossory, on 6 June 1592, about the new uniform of the students: 'They are all now apparelled like collegians, brave cloaks and threadbare

The *coleitor* at the nunciature in Lisbon, Fabio Biondi, also patriarch of Jerusalem, was actively concerned in the on-going financial maintenance of the college, and, three years after it was founded, he sought financial assistance for the new seminary. In a letter to Cardinal Aldo Brandini, dated 17 July 1593, he begs the cardinal to inform His Holiness of the difficulties of the 'poveri giovani Irlandesi fuggiti da quella Isola d'Irlanda per l'heresia'.[23] He further states: 'Io sono stato a visitarli, et sono restato molto sodisfatto di veder che in così poco tempo habbia fatto tanto progresso nelle lettere, et li Padri Gesuiti nelle lor scole gli attendono con molta carità. Stanno in certe povere case che tengono à pegione et con molta strettezza et necessità d'ogni cosa non havendo altro che venti scudi il mese da S. M.ta, diece de S. Alt.za et cinque dall'Archivescovo della Città, et certe altre poche provisioni che danno alcuni nobili.'[24] He also refers to de Melho da Silva in glowing terms. In December of the same year we find him thanking the cardinal for his good offices as regards the Irish students.

Some of the most noteworthy members of the Board were: 'o senhor conde Meirenho-Mor', 'D. Duarte de Castelo Branco', a member of a noble family with several important titles; 'o senhor Luís da Lencastre, comendador-mor de Aviz'. The surname Alemcastre (or Lencastre) is based on Lancaster and was a desirable one in Portugal, dating as it did from the English princess, Philippa of Lancaster, daughter of John of Gaunt. She became queen of Portugal in 1387 on her marriage to Dom João I, founder of the Aviz dynasty which ruled Portugal until 1580. Among her sons were the future King Duarte (Edward) and Prince Henry the Navigator. She is buried in the great abbey of Batalha, built by her husband. Luís de Lencastre was *comendador mayor* of Aviz and a great-grandson of Dom João II (1481–95), who died without a legitimate heir.[25]

---

purses. (Senhor) Garsia, our protector, has a good desire to maintain all, but he cannot get sufficient with all the diligence he uses,' ibid., p. 211; see also p. 204. Both these letters, in English, are from the Landowne Mss 71, number 49, Brit. Mus.,   **23** G. da C., pp 213–15. Translation: ' … poor young Irishmen who have fled from the island of Ireland because of heresy.'   **24** Ibid. Translation: 'I have visited (the college) and I have been very satisfied to see that in such a short time so much progress has been made in letters, and that the Jesuit Fathers in their school attend to (the students) with great charity. They are in certain poor houses, which they rent and suffer much scarcity and necessity with an income of only twenty *scudi* per month from His Majesty, ten from His Highness and five from the Archbishop of the city, and certain other small provisions from some nobles'. **25** See J.H. Saraiva, op. cit., pp 29–30, 200–1.

Gaspar de Sousa was the controller of the board (*provedor da mesa*), in 1600, and a future governor of Brazil.[26] Diego da Fonseca, Damião de Aguiar and Francisco Rebelho Conigzeo were three high-court judges, *desembargadores*.[27] Bras da Costa was treasurer of the board in 1593. Luís Rodrigues de Guevara was the secretary (*escrivão*) of the board and Francisco Frazão took over this office on the death of D. Luís. There were many other distinguished and influential people, who gave amounts for the upkeep of St Patrick's over the same period.[28]

The government of the college was transferred to the Jesuits from the board of *fidalgos* in 1605. The statutes of the college were also approved by the archbishop of Lisbon at that time. From that date the rector and officials of the college were, in the main, Irish Jesuits. However, from 1624 by royal ordinance from Madrid, no foreigner was permitted to be the head of a religious institution in the kingdom of Portugal.[29] The arrangements with São Roque and other locations for the housing of the college had been short-term and the Irish college once again found a wealthy patron and yet another 'founder' in 1611. Dom António Fernandes Ximenes, 'a nobleman of the household of His Majesty and resident of this city in the lands of the Ximenes family',[30] generously funded the purchase of 'sua propria casa', their own house: this was to be the building, which housed the college until its final closure in 1834.

Dom António had a document of endowment drawn up in 1611, giving the house to the college. It was his wish to perform 'huma obra pia, e de muito serviço de Nosso Senhor divino, e ajuda das almas, e em especial a redução de herejes seismáticos e exaltação da fé Cathólica'[31] The second contract, in 1616, gave funds for work, repairs and ornaments necessary for the college church[32] and refers to donations from 1616 to 1631 of many pieces of silver, ornaments and other items for use in the church as well as funds to buy a *quinta*, a small estate for the collegians, – all of these costing 20,000 *cruzados* – as declared in his will, made in 1630 and codicils

---

26 G. da C., pp 203–4. **27** Ibid. p. 234. **28** MT 1593–1600. See also G. da C., pp 203–4, 269; idem., 'St Patrick's school', p. 48. **29** MT 3 Feb. 1624. **30** ' ... fidalgo da casa de sua Magestade e morador nesta cidade no terreiro do Ximenes' (later called Largo do Caldas, G. da C., *Fontes*, p. 439). The family of the benefactor was very wealthy, among the richest merchants in Portugal, Italy: Low Countries and India: ibid., p. 434; DDA, file 117/7, Irish College of St Patrick, Lisbon, original endowment of the college, 1611. **31** Ibid. Translation: 'a pious work and of much service to Our Divine Lord, a help for souls and, in particular, for the reduction of heresy and exaltation of the Catholic Faith.' **32** Ibid.

made in 1631. Arrangements were also made for a sum to set up a chair of theology 'para sempre,' for ever. He adds that he would have liked to do more for the Irish priests, 'por sua muita virtude e firmeza na Nossa Santa Fe'[33] but he had obligations to his many poor relations. In his will, after many legacies for members of his family, there is a clause that, in the event of the college's ceasing to exist for any reason, the property should pass to the Dominican college of Corpo Santo and if it, too, had closed it should go to the nearest relative of his father, Tomás Ximenes, deceased.

Dom António further specified that his body was to be interred under the high altar in the Irish college. Certain sums of money were also earmarked for the poor, for widows, for prisoners and for the ransoming of captives in Moorish lands, particularly the most helpless, such as women and children. This charitable man, a bachelor, lived in the college for the last ten years of his life, dying aged sixty-eight on 13 February 1631.[34]

THE FOUNDATION MASSES

Most of what were termed the Obligatory or Foundation Masses for the principal founder, and eventually for other benefactors, were set up at this time. These masses were offered for the pious intentions of benefactors of the Irish college. Over the earlier years of the foundation, many charitable people in Lisbon showed their concern for the exiled clerical students by donating sums of money for the setting-up of the college. These monies were either for the initial purchase of the house, for repairs or decoration of the chapels within the main church, or for the maintenance and honorariums of the professors appointed to the chairs of theology and philosophy, as was the case with the principal benefactor, Dom António Fernandes Ximenes. Other benefactors came to the rescue of the college at different times. In return for the donations received, the collegian priests were obliged to offer specific numbers of masses for the repose of the souls of the donor and/or his relatives.

The principal donors of these masses,[35] which dated from the early seventeenth century, were: Dom António Fernandes Ximenes, on whose behalf two daily masses were to be said for his soul. Two daily masses were to be celebrated, by the collegiate priests, for the soul of Jerónimo Ximenes

---

33 Ibid. Translation: '... because of their great virtue and steadfastness in Our Holy Faith'.   **34** Ibid. and G. da C., p. 441.

de Aragão, brother of Dom António. He married twice and on the death of his second wife in 1630 he entered the Jesuit Order and also resided in St Patrick's College. He died aged eighty-five years on 27 June 1666.

Luís Fernandes de Almada requested that two daily masses be offered for his soul and that of his first wife, Isabel Gomez. His second wife, Cecilia de Lega, was also a generous benefactor of the college. Mass was to be offered, in perpetuity, for the souls of Paulo de Chaves, his father, his mother, Maria Vicente, and the rest of their dead. Thirteen masses were to be offered on the feasts of the Apostles and St Paul; on the feasts of Christ, Our Lady, St Anthony, St Vincent, St Valentine, and St Joseph; every year eight masses to be offered on All Saints Day, finishing on the last day of the Octave. Brites Roiz (or Rodrigues) made a donation for thirty masses to be celebrated annually for his soul. Cecilia de Lega, second wife of Dom Luís Fernandes de Almada, made mass donations for herself and her sister, D. Joana de Cruz, a deceased nun. They were the donors of a shrine, or chapel, dedicated to St John the Baptist, within the college chapel. Their offering was for one daily mass for both their souls. It is interesting to note that rents from some houses in Bairro Alto and rua das Esteiras were to supply the funds for these masses.

Ormizonda de Moraes asked that twenty masses be celebrated each year for the intentions and for the soul of the donor, 'pera sempre em quanto o mundo dura' – for ever, as long as the world endures. At a later stage institutions were released from these unrealistic obligations of masses to be offered in perpetuity. The college was also contracted to offer two masses of obligation annually in the church of Santa Ana Termo de Alenquer. As the number of students dropped over the years the obligatory masses often had to be celebrated outside the college, by priests who were not collegians which meant a drop in income for the college.

The listings of the celebrants of the contractual masses for the several *lisboetas*, named above, provide useful information on the dating of entrances and exits of many collegians. Contracts for the celebration of these masses were made by the donors and strict details of the offering of these masses were kept. For example, masses for Jerónimo Ximenes de Aragão were celebrated by twenty-six collegian priests, all named in the document, between 12 March 1673 and 31 December 1705, a span of thirty two years.[36]

35 LIS/2.   **36** Ibid; also see G. da C., pp 441–2.

FOUNDATION AND HISTORY

THE HOUSE

The residence bought on 21 November 1611 from the Discalced Carmelite fathers was described as some buildings in the Costa do Castelo region, attached to the St Crispin hermitage, 'purchased for the sum on 2 *contos* and 400 thousand *reis*'. It was described as a two-storey building (over the years two more floors have been added), the lower floor for the community and class rooms, and the upper one split by a wide corridor, including the washrooms and cubicles for the collegians. The entrance hall was paved with beautiful marble. At the back of it there was a painted stone cross, the work of the rector, António Vieira Senior (1686–90), who had been responsible also for the restoration of the country houses on the college estates.[37] This house was judged sufficient to maintain twelve collegians, although in 1592 the number rose to twenty-four. The house itself had a long and unusual history. Originally it was the *casa senhorial* (manor house) of one of the Noronha family – Dom Garcia de Noronha, a viceroy of India, who died in Goa sometime before 1566.[38] The Noronha family gave many members to the Indian service and was one of the wealthiest and most distinguished families in Portugal.

The office of Portuguese viceroy in India was not a well-paid one but it was, nonetheless, much sought after at that time. The reason for this was that the perquisites of the position were huge. There was so much competition for each of these that the offices, or reversions, were bought and sold, often, at public auction. It is recorded that in 1538 the viceroy of India, Dom Garcia de Noronha, 'publicly sold by auction every vacant appointment in Portuguese India' – an example followed in 1614 by the king himself.[39]

The viceroy's mansion in Lisbon had lain empty until it was bought in 1604 by the Discalced Carmelites from the viceroy's heirs. After residing there for seven years they sold it in 1611 to the benefactor of the Irish college, Dom António Fernandes Ximenes, who presented it to the Irish.

Since Dom António had wanted for some time to perform a work of much service to Our Lord, the buying of the house, and the donation of

---

37 G. da C., p. 98; the *conto* was equal to 1,000 *escudos*; *milreis* = 1,000 *reis* (*reis* is the plural of *real*). See C.R. Boxer, op. cit., p. 391.   **38** There were at least four viceroys in Goa in the sixteenth century named Noronha, according to the standard source for biographical data for Portugal and Brazil, *Grande Enciclopedia Portuguesa e Brasileira* (Lisboa, 1945). It is not clear which of them was the owner of the *casa senhorial*.   **39** *Encyclopaedia Britannica*, 13th edition, xxi–xxii (London,

it to a worthy cause, such as the foundation of a seminary for priests who would return to their country after training and combat heresy there, was just such a work of *misericórdia*. This kind of gesture was particularly common among New Christians (*cristianos novos*) in order to demonstrate their fidelity to their new religion. The family of António Fernandes Ximenes was of Jewish origin. In spite of being New Christians, the family was given the status of nobility in 1589.[40]

Despite the many 'founders' of the college, it would appear that the Irish Jesuits were extremely active from the beginning. Father Thomas White and Father John Howling were the prime movers in all matters relating to the setting-up of the institution.

THE LANDOWNE PAPERS

Nine letters which form part of the Lansdowne Manuscripts in the British Library have a curious history.[41] At the time when British pirates, including Lord Cumberland, Sir Walter Raleigh and Sir Francis Drake, were the terror of shipping in the seas to the west of Europe a certain vessel, a pinnace (*um pinaclo*), left Lisbon on a date in 1592, bound for a port in the north of Spain. It was taken by pirates somewhere between Lisbon and the coast of Galicia. On board this ship were several letters from Irish clerics in Lisbon addressed to members of the Irish community in Santiago de Compostela. It was customary for pirates to cast such mail into the sea.[42] For once, though, this did not happen. The captain of the marauding ship, one Samuel Stonley, for some reason held on to the letters and gave them to the mayor of Bristol, Walter Stansast, on his return to that port. The mayor sent them on 26 July 1592 (5 August according to the

---

1926), p. 145.   **40** The New Christians were often crypto-Jews, known as *marranos*, who were 'ostensibly faithful adherents of the Catholic Church [who] continued to practise Jewish rites in secret', José Hermano Saraiva, op. cit., p. 58; G. da C. pp 435–40.   **41** G. da C., pp 96–7.   **42** There are many examples of complaints about non-receipt of letters both in Pacific and Atlantic waters, where pirates preyed on shipping. Father Joannes Yate, an English Jesuit, who corresponded with some Irish Jesuits after he went to Brazil in 1593, had two of his letters intercepted: Hogan, op. cit., p. 31. The bishop of Cuzco, who was a friend and sponsor of Father Paul Sherlock, rector of the Irish College, Santiago de Compostela (1624–8), comments on the uncertainty of the post in Peru, in the early seventeenth century, too: *Salamanca letters*, p. 3.

[32]

New Calendar)⁴³ to Lord Burghley,⁴⁴ and, subsequently, they ended up in the British Museum.

The solemn inauguration of the Irish College of St Patrick took place on Pentecost Sunday, 1592. Some of the Irish priests present wrote later describing the ceremonies to their friends in Santiago de Compostela. The letters never arrived. Now preserved for posterity by an act of piracy, they give us a vivid picture of the important event. The reasons why the letters were delivered to the mayor of Bristol and passed on to Lord Burghley give an interesting slant on the intelligence system in operation in England at that time. The captain claims that his 'humble duty remembered' impels him to inform the 'right honorable sir ... that there is a semynarye, or Colledge, latelie erected at Luxborne for the Irishe natyon, discoveringe alssoe dyvers of their confederates, as by the said leters may appere'.⁴⁵ So, these dangerous and seditious Irish clerics, and their confederates, had to be watched and kept under surveillance ...

The contents of all the letters⁴⁶ are noteworthy, not for any trace of sedition or plotting, but because they throw some light on an event which was of great importance to the exiled churchmen – the formal opening of the Irish college at Lisbon. The subject matter of all nine letters is of interest but only two highlight the formal inauguration ceremony.⁴⁶ The earlier letter, dated 21 May 1592, was from John Howling to Patrick Sinnott, a priest friend, who lived in El Ferrol, Galicia. Written from St Anthony's, the Jesuit novitiate house in Lisbon, it is a chatty letter with snippets of news of various people from both the Irish and English *emigré* colony in Lisbon. The main theme is a description of the ceremony on Whit Sunday, 1592. The first mass, a sung mass, was celebrated by the primate of Ireland, Archbishop Edmund MacGauren, who became archbishop of Armagh in August 1587. On 25 January 1588, he was in Lisbon. He brought with him with great pomp and ceremony, a relic of a fragment of bone from the skull of St Brigid. He presided at the ceremony of the handing over of this precious, relic in its 'beautiful reliquary' in the

---

43 There was a difference of ten days between the Julian calendar and the Gregorian calendar adopted in Catholic countries following the brief of Gregory XIII in March, 1582. Protestant states did not adopt it until 1700.   **44** G. da C., pp 96–7. William Cecil Burghley, Lord Burghley (1521–98), became lord high treasurer of England in 1572 and was an influential statesman under Edward VI, Mary and Elizabeth.   **45** Ibid.   **46** The texts of the letters are published in G. da C., pp 202–11. The two relevant letters are British Museum, Lansdowne Mss

church of St Roque, the principal church of the Jesuits in Lisbon, designed by the Italian architect, Filippo Terzo, in the early sixteenth century.[47]

At the formal inauguration ceremony of St Patrick's, the primate blessed the house, and was reported to have been 'moved to tears of devotion' by the sermon (*propósito*) preached by the superior of St Roque. All the students and 'our noblemen were present, 'says Howling, but he was deeply hurt by the refusal of the bishop of Killaloe, Francis Cornelius Ryan, to attend the ceremonies: 'Laonese,[48] not any of his would come to our feast on Sunday last, the griefe of which will never go out of my heart'.

He returns to this subject in the second letter dated 26 May written to Bishop Thomas Strong of Ossory, who was a suffragan bishop of Santiago: 'The bishop of Killaloe refused to come to our feast and I may boldly say (as Willie Nougle[49] knows also) he has been and is, sooner a persecutor than a favourer of this poor congregation. God make him our friend and pardon his doing hitherto.'[50] Gonçalves da Costa interprets Ryan's antagonism to the college as 'racist'. The bishop came to Lisbon in September, 1582, and was active in promoting the Irish cause. There was at that time a rift between Old Irish and the Anglo-Irish, represented by the Jesuits on the latter side, and this is borne out by Domnall O'Sullivan Beare's attitude to them and the merchant class from Cork and Waterford whom he regarded as being pro-English.[51]

From 1605 to 1624 the college of St Patrick was ruled by Irish Jesuits – John Howling, Thomas White, Cornelius Roche, John Baptist Dugin, and William Magrath.[52] The college's management was taken over by Portuguese Jesuits in 1624, and this caused violent resistance amongst the collegians. It is recorded, that one Portuguese Jesuit, Dom Diego de Couto, was forcibly ejected by a *piquete,* or picket-guard.[53] Nine Portuguese rectors followed William Magrath in 1624, and in 1654 another Irish Jesuit, Edmund Kelly, took over for three years. Irrespective of the royal order of 1624 forbidding foreign superiors, few Irish Jesuits were available in

---

71, number 49, ff. 95–6 and 100–100v. **47** G. de C., p. 203. See also Roisín Ní Mheara, 'Sancta Brigida abroad: a tale of two cities', *Sea. AM* 18 (1999–2000) 49–65. In Portuguese sources St Brigid seems to have a crisis of identity; also, see G. da C., p. 26. **48** Laonese signifies diocese of Killaloe: G. da C., p. 205. **49** William Nogle (Nagle?) had been ordained by Bishop Ryan in 1589: G. da C., p. 209. **50** Ibid. **51** See Gareth Davies in *Catholic tastes and times: essays in honour of M.E. Williams*, edited by Margaret Rees (Leeds: Trinity and All Saints College, 1987), pp 98–9. **52** G. da C., p. 257. **53** Ibid. p. 256.

FOUNDATION AND HISTORY

Portugal at that time, most of them having returned to the Irish mission where they were active, but kept a low profile, and no other Irish rector appears between 1657 and 1755, when the terrible earthquake devastated Lisbon and the college was extensively damaged. On 1 November 1755, at about 10 a.m., when crowds had gathered in the capital's churches for the celebration of mass for All Saints Day, the first tremors of the earthquake were felt. The after-shocks continued for several weeks. After the first and worst shock a disastrous tidal wave engulfed Lisbon and many fires started all over the stricken city.

THE FINAL FATE OF THE BUILDING

Although the building was damaged in the earthquake, it survived as a college until about 1834, when it finally closed its doors to Irish seminarians. In compliance with one of the conditions of the founder back in the sixteenth century it was duly handed over to the Dominican Fathers of Corpo Santo. The Dominicans ceded it to various religious orders, but eventually it was sold in 1902 to the Sisters of St Joseph of Cluny. The Sisters had been renting the college for some years at an annual rent of 180,000,000 *escudos*.[54] The building was used for a time as a refuge for *rapazes desválidos* (destitute children), until its acquisition by the Sisters and conversion by them into their mother-house. It became a school for girls – in time considered one of the best in Lisbon. In 1910 it had such standing that 98 day-pupils from the most distinguished families of the capital attended it. At the same time a free school for 90 girls was also run in the former Irish college.[55]

When the republican regime came to power in Portugal in 1910 the Irish college building was handed over to the Ministry of Justice. It is now home to the law courts of the Tribunal Administrativo do Circulo de Lisboa.

Gonçalves da Costa, who has contributed so much to the study of the Irish in Portugal, has aptly described it as it was in 1989, and his description is appropriate even today:

> Quem desce do Castelo para a Sé, ainda encontra o grande imóvel do Colégio de São Patrício com o muro pombalino de tijolo, pedra miúda e argamassa a esboroar-se aos poucos ao longo das Escadinhas

54 Irish Dominican Archives, Corpo Santo, Envelope 43.   55 G. da C., p. 127.

de São Crispim. De pedra lavrada ostentando certo ar de nobreza, apenas uma janela arqueada e as silharias da porta principal, anteriores ao terramoto de 1755.[56]

However, it is a matter of pride for the Irish visitor that a plaque placed on the wall of the building tells us, in Irish, English and Portuguese, that this building once housed the exiled seminarians of Ireland.

---

[56] Ibid. p. 128. Translation: ' ... he who goes down from the Castle (of St George) to the Se still encounters the large building of the College of St Patrick with its Pombaline walls of brick, small stones and mortar rising gradually along the steps of St Crispin. Made of cut stone, displaying a certain air of nobility, only a single arched window and the outline of the principal door pre-date the earthquake of 1755.'

CHAPTER 3

The Administration of the College

THE RECTORS

A brief issued during the pontificate of Urban VIII (1623–44) conferred extraordinary power on the rector of an Irish college. This power, to present candidates for ordination, had hitherto been the preserve of the episcopate and its conferring on the rectors was an important milestone on the road to the provision of adequate numbers of priests to work in the field in the circumstances prevailing in Ireland at that time. It was a power that the Irish bishops strove hard and long to reclaim, when conditions improved with the relaxation of the Penal Laws.[1]

One instance of the problems arising from this power being exercised improperly is demonstrated by the action of a Portuguese Jesuit, Afonso de Mexia. Grave offence was caused by him for issuing dimissorial letters to John Verdon (not the bishop of Ferns) for ordination in 1686.[2] It appears that Mexia gave Verdon the letters so that he might be ordained without any testimony of the Ordinary. The letters were rejected by the vicar-general and canons of the metropolitan of Lisbon as invalid. Father de Mexia, knowing this and without the knowledge of the rector, offered the letters to the inquisitor general. John Verdon was duly ordained and when the vicar-general and canons heard this, they complained to the General of the Jesuits in Rome. In his correspondence with the provincial, the General took a very serious view of this matter and set up a firm line of investigation. He also suggested severe penalties if the matter should be proved against Mexia. Strangely, some years later, Mexia was made rector of the college, but his unorthodox methods finally caused his removal.

1 Tridentine law laid down that a bishop must authorise the ordination of a student to the diocesan priesthood. This would be through the issue of dimissorial letters by the prelate. Due to the exceptional circumstances in Ireland, however, Urban VIII, in 1623, permitted the ordination of students in the Irish continental colleges, on the authority of the rector, on the sole title of a mission in Ireland. See T.F. Walsh, op. cit., pp 14, 48–9, 77. **2** MT 9 Mar. 1686.

Walter French was the first Irish rector of the college of St Patrick in Lisbon. He was in bad health in 1592 at the formal opening of the college and was suffering from what he called 'this unfortunate fever'. He had been preceded by a Portuguese rector, whom John Howling described as a 'lapidator', presumably a dilapidator.[3] Howling expresses great delight that the 'lapidator' has gone and French has taken over. He says that French governed with 'great love and truth'. He reflects that 'if our nation had as much obedience as others have he were the fittest man for this purpose I know of our country abroad. But he is too mild for our nation. Yet, God be thanked, they live better under his government than before.'

From 1592 until 1606 the college was administered by a succession of Jesuits, some Irish, some Portuguese: João Delgado, Pedro de Fonseca, John Howling, João de Lucena, Cosme de Magalhães, Alvaro Lobo and Nicholas Leynich.[4] In 1606 Thomas White became rector, followed by three Irish rectors:

1606–9	Thomas White
1609–19	Cornelio da Rocha (Cornelius Carrick
1619–21	João Baptista Dugin (John Baptist Duggan)
1622–24	Guilhermo da Cruz (William Magrath)[5]

As already explained the rectorship of the college was assumed in 1624 by Portuguese Jesuits, by royal order from Madrid decreeing that no foreigner could be head of a religious institution in Portugal. From 1624 to the suppression of the Jesuits in 1759 the rectors were:

3 G. da C., p. 209. Father John Howling wrote from Lisbon, on 26 May 1592, to Bishop Thomas Strong of Ossory, suffragan archbishop of Santiago de Compostela, stating: 'We had a Portugal rector (I may say lapidator).' Although the form of the word he used was lapidator he, presumably, meant 'dilapidator' or 'one who causes ruin'.   **4** Ibid. p. 256. John Howling was born in Wexford c.1542 and entered the Jesuit novitiate c.1573. He spent time in Spain and was finally sent to Lisbon in 1588. He wrote an account of the Irish martyrs, who died between 1578 and 1588. He was involved in the setting-up of the Irish College, Lisbon, from its infancy. He died ministering to the people of Lisbon during the plague of 1599. Another victim was his great friend, Father Pedro Fonseca. See Hogan, op. cit., pp 29–47. Nicholas Leynich was born in 1567 in Clonmel. He joined the Jesuits in 1590, studied Humanities at St Anthony's College, Lisbon. After further studies he joined the staff of St Patrick's College, where he acted as minister and confessor, until he left for Ireland in 1598: G da C., pp 226–9, 428.   **5** Thomas White, born at Clonmel

THE ADMINISTRATION OF THE COLLEGE

Álvaro Tavares, 1624–6
Manuel Vieira, 1626–9
Nuno da Cunha, 1634–6
João Martins, 1636–7
Diego Pereira, 1637
Francisco Amaral, 1638–41
Baltasar Teles, 1641–5
Manuel Mascarenhas, 1646–9
Miguel Tinoco, 1649–54
Edmund Kelly, 1654–7
Manuel Monteiro, 1658
António de Barros, 1659–60
Pedro Peixoto, 1660–4
João de Sousa, 1665–8
João Gomes, 1669–71
Domingo Lousado, 1671–8
Benito Pereira, 1675–7
Luís Nogueira, 1678–80
Francisco Caldeira, 1680–2
Manuel Soares, 1682–6
António Vieira Senior, 1686–90
Afonso de Mexia, 1690–2
Francisco Taveres, 1692–5

João de Faria, 1695–8
Manuel dos Reis, 1698–1702
Manuel Martins, 1702–5
João Franco, 1705–8
Manuel Gomes, 1708–11
Agostinho da Cunha, 1711–12
José de Almeida, 1712
António Carneiro, 1717
Antonius de Sousa, 1720
António Carneiro, 1725–8
vice-rector Francisco de Figueredo, 1729–42
Francisco Taveres, 1733
Inácio Vieira, 1734
António de Faria, 1737
Josephus Falcão, 1738–42
António Pessoa, 1742–3
Manuel de Silva, 1743
Luís Alberto, 1745–8
Manuel da Silva, 1748–53
Francisco Ribeiro, 1753–7
Nuno da Cunha, 1757–9.[6]

in 1556, entered the Society in 1588. He is also credited with the foundation of several of the other Irish Colleges and was rector of Salamanca, Lisbon and Santiago de Compostela. He came from a distinguished Anglo-Irish Catholic family in Clonmel. He died on 28 May 1622. See Hogan, op. cit., pp 48–70. Cornelius (da Rocha) MacCarrick was born in 1571 in Lochbulgen, diocese of Kilfenora. He attended the Irish College, Lisbon, entered the Society in 1601 and studied at the University of Coimbra. He was rector and minister in the college and returned to Ireland in 1624: G. da C., p. 237; LIS/4. John Baptist. Duggan, born 1584, was from either the diocese of Ossory, or Killaloe. He studied Latin, Philosophy and Theology at the Irish College. He entered the Society in 1603, and returned to Ireland in 1622: G. da C., pp 424–5. William Magrath was born in 1591 in Burges, south-west of Cahir, in the diocese of Cashel. He taught Philosophy in Coimbra and died 1651: G. da C., pp 423–4; LIS/4. **6** The names of the Portuguese rectors are included here, because of their importance as signatories of various petitions, including those for ordination, and of other

The rectorships during the period to 1759 were relatively short. In 1654 an Irishman, Edmund Kelly, from the diocese of Clonfert, was appointed rector, succeeding some ten Portuguese rectors, who governed in the intervening years. He ruled until 1657 and was the last Irish rector to hold office until the re-opening of the college in 1778, twenty-three years after the earthquake and nearly twenty years after the suppression of the Jesuits in Portugal in 1759. Nuno da Cunha administered the college after the earthquake and the subsequent turmoil caused by the damage to the city, until the expulsion of the Jesuit order from Portugal. The suppression of the Jesuits was during the government of the country by the Marquês de Pombal and it was during his regime that the Irish college was closed and confiscated.[7] Pombal was responsible for the re-building of the city after the earthquake and for many reforms in government. He has been described as a Jekyll-and-Hyde character by C.R. Boxer, the English scholar who has written extensively about Portuguese history.[8] Pombal profoundly affected his country for both good and evil. He ruthlessly suppressed the Jesuits and appeared to have had 'a pathological hatred' of the Society and a belief that the Order possessed immense wealth in gold and that if he confiscated their properties he would find this wealth. His phobia had become the maniacal obsession which it remained for the rest of his life.[9] It must have been a great disappointment to him that he found nothing of the sort.

An anonymous author[10] tells us that, after the earthquake, the Portuguese rector in charge at that time 'perhaps from age or natural timidity, showed much weakness in a trying hour,' and told the students of the college to 'flee the dangers'. It must be remembered that about 10,000 people had perished in the first shock. Many people, including the royal family, camped out of doors for many weeks after the first shock. However, the rector was told by the students that they knew 'full well their danger, but were resolved rather to die than to go back to Ireland without having accomplished the great end for which they had left home and kindred'.[11]

---

correspondence in the records: G. da C. pp 101–2; G. da C., 'St Patricks school' pp 39–40.　**7** The royal order for the confiscation of the property of the Society of Jesus was dated 19 January 1759, and the sequestration of the properties of St Patrick's College, its *feitorias* (goods), farms and houses, followed shortly afterwards. A minute inventory of everything, including personal property of staff and collegians, was made then: G. da C. op. cit, p. 123.　**8** The *Portuguese seaborne empire*, 1415–1825 (Manchester, 1991), pp 186–9.　**9** Boxer op. cit., p. 186. **10** *IER* 8 (1871), p. 309.　**11** Ibid.

THE ADMINISTRATION OF THE COLLEGE

The most vociferous in resisting the suggestion that they leave Portugal were Bartholomew Sherlock, later parish priest of St Catherine's, Meath Street, Dublin, and Michael Daly (sometimes mistakenly referred to as Brady) who was destined to play a major role in the restoration of the college to the Irish. The students, eight in number, withdrew to their *quinta*, on the outskirts of Lisbon, given to them by a generous benefactor in the seventeenth century, but it, too, had been ruined in the quake. They camped out of doors while the rector went by mule each morning to the Ajuda Palace, in Belém, where the royal family and the court were living in tents. The sole object of the poor man was to obtain a royal order for the removal of the students. This permission would, doubtless, have been forthcoming, but the Irish students, having been warned of the possible outcome, appealed to the king's confessor and a royal order was issued that the rector should stay in charge of the college[12] and the students should be sent to Évora to finish their course. In fact, many of the students had for years continued their studies at the universities of Coimbra and Évora.

The Irish College in Lisbon re-opened in 1778 largely due to the efforts of Father Michael Daly, who had worked ceaselessly for twenty years for the return of the college and some of the other property which had been confiscated. He stated in one of his letters to Bishop Troy of Ossory, and later of Dublin, that he had 'reason to think that the confiscation would not have taken place in our house, had any Irishman been on the spot'. Father Daly was named as rector on 30 April 1778 by royal decree, with the Board of Conscience (Mesa de Consciência) being given the power of inspection. He quickly applied to the Treasury for liquidation of the college's affairs which took a year to complete.[13]

Father Daly was succeeded in 1799 by Dr Bartholomew Crotty, who governed the college until 1811, when he returned to Ireland. He became parish priest of Cloyne and took charge of a small seminary there. Dr Crotty had been one of the earliest students to enrol in the re-established college after it opened, and had also served on the staff as a professor for almost twenty years. He was elected president of St Patrick's College, Maynooth (1813–33). On 11 June 1833, he became bishop of Cloyne (1833–46). He died on 4 October 1846, and was buried in the convent chapel in Midleton, Co. Cork.[14]

The Peninsular War caused the closure of the college once again. Dr John Dunn (O'Dunn) became rector after the departure of Dr Crotty and

12 Ibid. pp 310–1.   **13** DDA., a letter, dated 1 June 1780 from Father Daly to Archbishop Troy.   **14** McDonald, *IER* 8 (1872) p. 312.

was himself followed in 1823 by Father Hyacinth Joyce. The college, finally closed its doors to students in 1834. The last rector was Father Patrick Murray.[15] William McDonnell met him in the college in 1839. The foundation of St Patrick's College in Maynooth in 1795 and, later, the granting of Catholic Emancipation in 1829, spelled the end of the the Irish College, Lisbon, which had supplied priests to many Irish dioceses for a period of over three hundred years and was the *alma mater* of many of the priests of the penal times.

THE COLLEGE STAFF

Perhaps the most important position in the seminary after that of rector was the *ministro* and his duties were manifold. He dealt directly with the students. He was, in addition, responsible for the education of the boarders, the *convictores*, at the college. The boarders also attended classes at St Anthony's College, the novitiate of the Jesuit order in Lisbon. He was also required to monitor their progress.

In 1592 Walter French had a minister whose Christian name was Robert.[16] Cornelio da Rocha was procurator for a time after he had been rector. He was, apparently, blamed for not being able to control the disturbances in the college in 1624, and as a result was forced to return to Ireland. John Baptist Duggan, who had earlier returned to Ireland, was now requested to come back to Lisbon to replace him, but the Irish superior refused to release him for this purpose. He was noted by the Portuguese Jesuits for his religious spirit, zeal and good sense.[17]

The minister undoubtedly needed to be a man of many parts. The earliest minister I have identified, Peter Nash, was just such a man. He performed the role for thirty-five years, from 1614 to 1649, with complete success. He also served, with equal aplomb, as procurator for eighteen of these years from 1631 to 1649.[18] Peter Nash was born in 1581, in Fethard, Co. Tipperary, diocese of Cashel. He was a son of William Nash and Elena Molroney. He studied humanities at the Irish College, Lisbon, and also at the Irish College, Salamanca. He joined the Jesuit Order in Coimbra in 1607 and studied theology for two years before coming to live at St Patrick's, Lisbon, in 1613. He also spent some time at the University of

---

15 See Chapter 7.   **16** G. da C., *Fontes*, p. 204.   **17** Ibid., p. 100.   **18** LIS/6; G. da C., p. 99.

Évora. He was known as Father Ignatius within the college. He remained in St Patrick's until his death, sometime between 1649 and 1654.[19]

Other distinguished Irish ministers were Francis White, who succeeded Nash in 1649 and held the office until 1658. He was born in Waterford on 16 March 1617, and entered the Jesuit Order, graduating as an MA from the University of Coimbra. He returned to the Irish mission in 1667 and taught Greek, Hebrew and moral theology in Waterford, where he died in 1697.[20] Robert Neville was minister from 1660 to 1662. He was born on 5 July 1626. He received his early ecclesiastical education at St Patrick's College. He was ordained in 1655 and entered the Jesuit Order the same year. When his term of office ended he went to Madeira and died there fifteen years later.[21] He was succeeded by Richard Carew, who had a very distinguished career in the Jesuit order. He was born in 1619, entered the Jesuits in 1639 and became a brilliant theologian and professor in both Europe and the Azores. In 1659 he accompanied the Jesuit, Father de Magistris, to Brazil and stayed there for three years. He returned to Portugal in 1662 and four years later was sent to Ireland. He died in Waterford in 1690.[22] His successor was Augustinus Geraldinus, Augustine Fitzgerald. Born in Waterford on 6 April 1632, he entered the Society in 1655. He was minister for twelve years, from 1663 to 1675 and also taught theology in the college.[23]

Mathew White held the office of minister from 1678 to 1681. He was from the diocese of Cashel, was a student in the Irish College and studied at the University of Évora. He served as a preacher in Funchal and Évora and died in Oporto on 18 November 1700.[24] George Gelarte, an English Jesuit, was appointed minister from 1686 to 1690. The General of the Jesuit Order in Rome expressed misgivings about appointing an Englishman, given the Irish reputation for touchiness on the nationality of their rectors on previous occasions. In a letter to the provincial of the Jesuits in Lisbon he says, that he knows that Gelarte is not Irish but English and may not be acceptable to the seminarians. He need not have worried, Gelarte appears to have been quite acceptable.[25]

19 An unpublished work, compiled by Father Francis Finegan SJ, '*A biographical dictionary' of Irish Jesuits in the time of the Society's third Irish mission, 1598–1773*, p. 119. This work is in the Irish Jesuits Archives, Dublin. In the foreword, the author pays tribute to the 'splendid apparatus bequeathed by Father MacErlean to the Irish Province – the MacErlean Transcripts' which, he says, 'has rendered obsolete much of the writing of Hogan and Foley.' **20** Ibid., p. 206. **21** Ibid., p. 122. **22** G. da C. p. 421. **23** Ibid. p. 426; LIS/4. **24** G. da C., p. 326. **25** MT 29 Nov. 1687–Thyrsus Gonzalez to Vaz.

THE IRISH COLLEGE AT LISBON

Names of teachers are recorded from time to time. One of the earliest teachers was James Everard, son of Redmond Everard, who was born 1578 in Fethard, County Tipperary. He studied humanities at St Patrick's, finished his degree in philosophy and theology at the University of Coimbra and from 1592 onwards presided over the Philosophical arguments in St Patrick's College. He taught at the college, when it officially opened in 1592. He died at Cashel on Good Friday, 1646. His brother, Sir John Everard, was Speaker of the House of Commons.[26]

Cornelio de S Patricio (O'Mahony) taught moral theology in 1639, and was in 1625 prefect of studies for the theology and philosophy students.[27] Guilielmo da Cruz taught Latin from 1612 to 1617 and theology from 1620 to 1621,[28] Edmund Ennis held the chair of theology in 1636[29] and Robert Bath, who was twenty-eight years old in 1611 and already seven years as a religious, was sent from Rome to act as spiritual prefect.[30] Edmund Kelly was prefect of theologians and philosophers in 1625. He was also spiritual prefect in 1629 and was, of course, rector for a spell. He taught moral theology and scholasticism in 1639 and was chairman of the theological debates.[31]

The records available become very fragmentary at the end of the seventeenth century and I have found no Irish names on the staff after 1693. The college was run as a Portuguese Jesuit college with increasing numbers of boarders and, apparently, ever-decreasing numbers of Irish clerical students enrolling. This state of affairs continued until the suppression of the Jesuit order in 1759 and the closure of the college. When the college was eventually returned in 1778 the Irish were once again in control.

It also appears that after the Portuguese Jesuits took over the government of the college in 1624 the numbers of officers increased. The administration became top-heavy, with the Jesuit personnel almost equalling the numbers of collegians. By 1686, for example, there were seven or eight officers – a rector, two lecturers on Controversies, a consultor, a minister, a spiritual prefect, a

---

26 Finegan, op. cit., pp 52–3.   **27** Cornelius O'Mahony was born Muskerry in 1598 and studied in Seville, Coimbra and Évora. He was professor of moral theology in the University of Évora. He spent some time in the Azores and was there, in Ponta Delgada, when there was a bad earthquake in September 1630. He wrote many learned works on theology. He died in 1656. See G. da C., op. cit., pp 57–9.   **28** He was a former rector, William Magrath; see footnote 5.   **29** G. da C., p. 425.   **30** Bath was from County Meath; see G. da C. p. 247.   **31** He was from the diocese of Clonfert, and entered the Society in January 1623. He studied at Évora and was ordained in 1632: G. da C., pp 427–8.

THE ADMINISTRATION OF THE COLLEGE

procurator and, sometimes, two temporal coadjutors – while the students at that time totalled thirteen, with, in addition, two boarders.

The archbishops of Ireland complained on many occasions about the expropriation of their rights, and in 1731 also informed the General in Rome that there were too many Jesuits in the Lisbon college, while there was a scarcity of priests in Ireland. They did concede that the Jesuits had done a good job in running the college and commended them, because there the students acquired a knowledge of the vernacular language and 'other things useful in our country'. They also pointed out, that the students tended to forget their vernacular abroad, and that because of this 'Ireland suffers much'.[32] The question of the Irish language in the continental colleges comes to the surface from time to time in the 1650s, mainly in France.[33] It does not commonly occur in the Spanish or Portuguese establishments, which makes this matter of special interest in the Portuguese context.

In the seventeenth century another official is often listed among the personnel of the college. It was, of course, customary for clerics in those times to travel in pairs and, according to the rules of the Order, the rector of St Patrick's had *um companhero*, who accompanied him on all his visits outside the college. For example, Luke Wadding, a member of the Franciscan order, also had a travelling companion. Thomas White had several *companheros* over the years, since he was an inveterate traveller – for example, João de Moura in 1608 – and the rector, William Magrath, was accompanied on his duties by Thomas Nevin in 1623. The names of these *companheros* are sometimes given in the official lists of members of the college in the early years and are to be found in the *Catalogi brevii*, which are a rich source of information about the personnel of the college.[34]

COURSE OF STUDY

Before they had their own premises, and prior to the setting-up in St Patrick's, of the two chairs of philosophy and theology, the students attended lectures in grammar, humanities, science and philosophy in St Anthony's School. The Chairs had been instituted by the benefactor António Fernandes de Ximenes, and provision was made in his will to this

---

32 MT 20 Feb. 1731, letter from the Bishops of Ireland, Armagh, Dublin, Kildare, Ferns and Cashel to Francis Retz.   **33** T.F. Walsh, op. cit., pp 150–1, 159–60.   **34** The *Catologi brevii* are in LIS/4 and 6.

end. These chairs were of *Prima (Moral)* and *Vespera (Controversias)* and were designed to enable the students to respond to the objections of the Protestants.[35] In 1606 a special course was started in Coimbra, subsidized by the Court for the collegians of St Patrick's, many of whom went there to finish their courses.

The Colégio da Purificação was founded in 1579 by Cardinal Dom Henrique in the University of Évora for the education of secular priests as laid down by the Council of Trent. In it the king supported fifty students – three of whom could be foreigners. In fact, the number of foreigners often exceeded that figure, and many of these were Irish, who took their degrees and, in some cases, later became bishops in Ireland in '*aquela aflita igreja*'.[36] Indeed, one might be excused for thinking that the Colégio da Purificação was, in fact, an Irish college.

The degrees conferred in Coimbra and Évora were *bacharelat*, *mestre*, and *doctorão*. The standards were high and the requirements for these degrees were stringent. In all the *atos* relating to higher degrees the student had to defend a thesis and reply to objections and the courses of study took at least four years Many Irish received doctorates, with the highest honours, *cum laude*. C.R Boxer in his monumental study, *The Portuguese seaborne empire, 1415–1825*, is less than enthusiastic about the standards of courses in Coimbra and elsewhere in Portugal, but he professes the same doubts about those of Oxford and Cambridge.

On 21 July 1790, Father Daly, writing to Bishop Troy, invites him to send a candidate to the college immediately. Although the new course would not begin until October 1791, he says that he could find useful employment for him in the meantime. His instructions are, that he should bring a bed, sheets and blankets for his own use, a good stock of strong linen, underwear, shoes, stockings and waistcoats. He adds that what is durable and strong is what is required, as nothing fine is allowed. 'Most of these young fools lay out money on fine cloth in the dress and make their appearance in ruffled shirts, which they cannot use here.'[37] Most importantly, he usually tells prospective collegians to bring whatever books they had in Latin, Greek, particularly a lexicon, English or any language they might have studied.

---

35 G. da C., p. 260.   **36** Ibid., p. 385. Translation: 'in that afflicted Irish Church' See Chapter 4 re bishops who were collegians in St Patrick's.   **37** DDA, letter, 21 July 1790, Daly to Troy.

THE ADMINISTRATION OF THE COLLEGE

Father Daly, in a reply on 27 August 1795, to a letter dated July from Dr Troy, writes regarding a copy of the archbishop's pastoral letter and proposed legislation in the British parliament regarding the probability of what he called 'not total emancipation' but of some liberty being 'granted for the propagation of learning amongst our people'. He affirms that the 'restriction laid on it by Law is the most barbarous and inhuman of all their penal laws'.[38]

In his next letter, he continues the subject of his interest in the possibilities of legislation affecting education in Ireland. Having read newspapers and pamphlets, he feels that there are strong hopes that

> our emancipation, as it is termed, is not far distant; and it would seem, the fever of our slavery is coming to a crisis. What I long for is the Act of Parliament itself for the projected establishment for Catholic Education. I hope it is done with a liberality of Sentiment and fund that will render it really useful, and such as will answer all our wants in that line. If this is the case, we may shut up our doors on this side of the Water; as I suppose no one will seek abroad with inconvenience, what he can conveniently find at home.[39]

Prophetically, perhaps, he continues,

> I often considered ... whether the ceasing of persecution might not cause among us a greater falling off from Faith. Though I came to no conclusion on that head, yet I remain with apprehension about it. If this should be the event, if when men obtain from God these temporal blesssings, for which they so long sighed & often prayed, they then become ungrateful & forgetful of their Benefactor, what more absurd perverseness? Yet History shews, it is not unparalleled. May our People see in a true light what they owe Divine Goodness.[40]

There were undoubtedly many advantages received over the centuries through the support and generosity of Spain, Portugal and other Catholic countries of Europe which provided for the education of Irish clergy in Penal times. Our debt to these nations is enormous, both in spiritual and

---

38 Ibid. letter, same to same, 18 April 1795. **39** Ibid., same to same, 11 July 1795. **40** Ibid.

economic terms. These areas need study and there are many questions to be answered about the content, quality and effectiveness of the education offered.

For many centuries the people of Ireland needed champions and protectors as well as pastors: and, often, the returned priest was expected to fill these roles. Whether that was his function is irrelevant: that was what he was often asked to do. Was his training fitted to these needs? Did the clerical education offered in the two staunchly Catholic countries, Spain and Portugal, fit the priests for the task of ministering to a people denied education for centuries, and living in an environment which was, not only spiritually and ethnically alien to them, but openly hostile? Did their training give them the necessary tools to debate, to counter or to refute the teachings of the established church in Ireland or to counteract the rewards offered by conforming to it? Doubtless the courses followed in Spain and Portugal were suitable to those countries where Church and State were, if not in constant harmony, of like mind. In both countries there was orthodoxy and conformity. Heresy was kept at bay. Some would say the Inquisition saw to that. Back in Ireland there was official bigotry towards, suspicion of and downright hostility to the 'popish' priests.

The General of the Jesuit Order in Rome, Francis Retz, wrote on 10 November 1737, to Thomas Hennessy, superior of the Order in Clonmel, 'regarding the serious complaints from various provinces that had come to my notice concerning the very intractable inclination of those youths, who have been received into the Society and who are wanting in many of the requisite qualities'.[41]

Thomas Hennessy SJ, had complained to the General, that youths were being admitted to St Patrick's by the Portuguese provincial without his, Hennessy's, knowledge.[42] This was an on-going problem for the superior. The General apparently asked the provincial why this was being done. Possibly due to the reply received from him Retz counter-attacked by pointing out to Hennessy that there were serious complaints from various provincials concerning the intractable inclinations of those being sent to the seminaries.[43]

Hennessy's reply is interesting. He claims to have 'spared no effort in choosing candidates' and points out that 'no-one should be surprised that they are inferior to those brought up in countries of the Faith to show due

---

41 MT 10 Nov. 1737.   42 Ibid., 17 Nov. 1736.   43 Ibid., 10 Nov. 1737.

obedience, which heresy ever hates and has destroyed, not only amongst its own followers but also amongst all others, who live with heretics.'[44]

Hennessy's theory, which was a sign of the times, is based on the belief that since the heretics had thrown over their obedience to the authority of the pope, their behaviour and those, such as the Catholics, forced to live under their domination were infected with disobedience to authority of any kind. Was this belief held generally amongst Catholics at that time? Was it expressed by others in debate, and is there any basis for the belief? Was it copper-fastened by later events, such as the French Revolution and the fall-out from it, and other movements which questioned all authority except the people, and led us to what has been called 'the tyranny of the masses'?

Inevitably the education received by the Irish collegians in Spain and Portugal must have had an influence on the Church in Ireland. The training of Irish clerical students in France, for example, during the seventeenth and eighteenth centuries is sometimes blamed for the so-called Jansenistic tendencies of the Church in Ireland even into the nineteenth century. What were the tendencies in the Irish Church which might be imputed to the training in Iberia? In addition to the dearth of historical research on the history of the Irish colleges on the continent of Europe, already noted, there is another totally neglected area of study, namely, the subject of the education or training of the Irish clerical students in Spain, Portugal and elsewhere during those troubled times, and the impact of that training subsequently on the thinking of the Irish population in general. The most significant question concerns the influences which accrued and in the light of these, what tendencies might be attributed to that education? Further research on these aspects of the history of the continental colleges network will doubtless clarify these questions, which await the attention of the present generation of historical researchers.

---

44 Ibid., 2 Mar. 1738.

CHAPTER 4

The Bishops

When news of the election, as bishop of Ferns, of a former student of the Irish College, Salamanca, reached that college in August, 1745, it was celebrated with six dozen rockets or fireworks, such displays being customary at the time in thanksgiving or in celebration of a triumph.[1] Although, I have found no written evidence of similar jubilation whenever a former collegian of St Patrick's College, Lisbon was raised to the episcopate in Ireland, there were some grounds for such celebrations. At least fifteen former members of the college became prelates, some others vicars-general, who in many cases kept the show on the road, as it were, when it was not possible for a prelate to return to his diocese. Dr Nicholas Sweetman, the bishop of Ferns (1745–86) in question, certainly spent some time in Salamanca and his elevation in 1745 was celebrated there in fitting style. However, he was ordained in Lisbon on 18 September 1717.[2] He came to Salamanca two years earlier from the Irish College, Santiago de Compostela, and took the usual oath administered to the students on 6 July 1715. There is also a note appended to the record of his oath, dated 4 September 1721, to the effect, that 'when he should have become a priest', he would offer his masses for the rector's intentions. He was an exile in Spain for many years and was auxiliary to the archbishop of Santiago de Compostela.[3]

Michael Rossiter, an earlier bishop of Ferns (1698–1709), was also ordained at Lisbon on 27 December 1671.[4] He was successor, as bishop, to Luke Wadding (1684–98) – not to be confused with the famous Franciscan. His own successor was Dr John Verdon (1709–29), ordained in Lisbon 17 August 1676, who had a distinguished career at the University of Évora, where he was conferred with a doctorate, *cum duplici laude*, on 19 January 1687.[5]

Four former students, Peter Talbot SJ, Patrick Russell, John Linegar and John Carpenter, became in turn archbishop of Dublin. Peter Talbot (1669–80) was from Carton, near Maynooth. He is described as a man 'of

---

1 Denis O'Doherty, *Arch. Hib.* 4 (1915) 31.   **2** Fenning, 2, p. 75.   **3** D.J. O'Doherty, loc. cit., p. 5.   **4** Fenning, 2, p. 74.   **5** Ibid. p. 76; G. da C., pp 54, 416.

fine talent, good judgment and prudence, more choleric than phleghmatic'.[6] He was a student of the Irish College, Lisbon, until he entered the Jesuits in 1635, aged 17 years. He received a doctorate from the University of Coimbra and subsequently taught Latin in St Anthony's, in Lisbon, until his name disappears from the records. He returned to Ireland, where he died in prison in 1680. He is said to have received Charles I into the Church.

Dr Patrick Russell (1683–92) was ordained in Lisbon on 12 June 1654.[7] After the battle of the Boyne (1690) he left for the continent, where he died. John Linegar (1734–92) became a priest on New Year's Eve, 1694, in the Convento do Carmo, which was almost totally destroyed in the 1755 earthquake.[8] Dr John Carpenter (1770–86) took holy orders on 18 June 1752.[9] In March 1764, Carpenter travelled to Lisbon on behalf of the Irish bishops, regarding the confiscation of the Irish College in Pombal's time. His mission was not successful and it is said that Pombal was unfriendly towards him.[10] Roccus MacGeoghegan OP, bishop of Kildare and Leighlin (1629–44), studied at Lisbon, when he was thirteen years old. He went on to Salamanca to finish his studies.[11]

Archbishop Thomas Walsh of Cashel (1626–54) was also a student in Lisbon before going to Salamanca in 1602.[12] Dr Eustace Brown was bishop of Killaloe from 1713 to 1724. He was ordained on 24 September 1672. He received a doctorate at the University of Évora, *cum laude*, on 31 December 1681.[13] In the 1704 register he is recorded as living in Emly. Dr Patrick Kelly (1822–9), bishop of Waterford, was also an *alumnus* of the Irish College, Lisbon,[14] as was Dr Patrick Comerford of Waterford (1629–52). Could John Murphy, ordained in Lisbon on 10 May 1795, have been the bishop of Cork (1815–47).[15]

The West of Ireland was represented by John de Burgo, archbishop of Tuam (1647–66) and bishop of Clonfert from 1641 to his transfer to Tuam, who was ordained in Lisbon from St Patrick's College[16] on 23 May 1621. Archbishop de Burgo studied in St Patrick's before going on to the

---

6 'muito bom engenho, bom juizo e prudencia, mais colérico que fleumático': G. da C., p. 432. **7** LIS/8; Fenning, 1, p. 116. **8** Fenning, 2, p. 69. **9** Ibid., 3, p. 144. **10** See Hugh Fenning, 'The archbishops of Dublin, 1693–1786' in James Kelly and Dáire Keogh (eds) *History of the Catholic diocese of Dublin* (Dublin, 2000), p. 207. **11** He was born in Moycashel, County Westmeath. See Denis O'Doherty, *Arch. Hib.* 2 (1913) 11–12. **12** LIS/4; O'Doherty, *Arch. Hib.* 2 (1913) 13; G. da C., p. 415. **13** Fenning, 2, p. 63; G. da C., op. cit p. 54. **14** O'Boyle, op. cit., p. 180; G. da C., p. 416. **15** Fenning, 3, p. 152. **16** LIS/7; G. da C., op.

University of Évora. Nicholas Skerritt, archbishop of Tuam (1580–3), was forced to flee to Lisbon and died there in 1583.[17]

Another important Connachtman was James Fallon, vicar-general of Clonfert, and later bishop of Ossory (1669–95), who was ordained in Lisbon 21 July 1615.[18] Walter Lynch was bishop of Clonfert from 1647 to 1664 and was ordained in Lisbon some time before 1625.[19]

Several exiled prelates lived and died in Lisbon in the sixteenth and seveenth centuries. These were not former students of St Patrick's College, but are recorded here as Irishmen, who either carried out their duties in Lisbon, some as assistant-bishops or otherwise, or who may have had a more temporary association with the city. Gonçalves da Costa claims that there were at least twenty-six prelates in Portugal in the period, 1575–1712 – some passing through, others with the status of exiles. Some early bishops who passed through Lisbon or spent time there in the mid-sixteenth century were Thomas O'Herlihy, of Ross (1561–80), Donald MacCongail, of Raphoe (1562–89), Eugene O'Hart OP, of Achonry (1562–1603) and Donal Ó Teig, of Armagh (1560–2), all returning from consecration in Rome, and the first three also from the closing stages of the Council of Trent. Redmond O Gallagher, of Killala (1545–69) stopped in Lisbon on his way to Rome in 1565 and was unable to go any further. He stayed there for a while and helped the archbishop of Lisbon at the royal chapel. He returned home and was murdered by English soldiery, aged 70.[20] Andrew O Crean OP, of Elphin (1562–94) also visited the city on his way to Rome. Thomas Strong, of Ossory, has already been mentioned. He too was an exile in Spain but kept in touch with the clergy in Lisbon. He was co-adjutor to the archbishop of Santiago de Compostela and died there in 1601.

Two prominent churchmen, Cornelius O'Mulryan (Ryan) OFM, of Killaloe (1576–1616) and David Kearney of Cashel (1603–25) both lived for some years in Lisbon, where they ordained Irish seminarians, Ryan in the years 1587 to 1611 and Kearney, a small number, between 1618 and 1621. The archbishop of Lisbon, Dom Miguel de Castro, accepted Ryan as his 'ringed' bishop. He died in the Franciscan monastery of Jesus and was buried there in 1616.[21] Archbishop Kearney died in Rome in 1625. One of the best-known and best-loved historical figures in the troubled history of the period under review is the Franciscan, Father Luke Wadding, who also

cit., p. 410.   **17** He is not recorded as a student of St Patrick's.   **18** Fenning, I, p. 110.   **19** LIS/4.   **20** Ibid. G. da C., pp 28, 132; O'Boyle, op. cit., p. 182.   **21** Fenning, I, p. 106; G. da C., p. 209.

enrolled at St Patrick's College when very young.²² Edmund MacGauran, archbishop of Armagh (1587–93), was another early resident of Lisbon, he presided at the ceremonies when the relics of St Brigid were taken in Processsion to the church of São Roque in 1588.

The exiled bishop of Kilmore, Michael MacDonagh OP (1728–46), who had returned to Ireland to occupy his bishopric, was captured and imprisoned in 1739. He escaped to Lisbon where he died in November 1746 aged only 48 years and was buried in Corpo Santo.²³ The bishop of Cork, Cloyne and Ross, John Baptist Sleyne (1693–1712), was another exile who lived in Lisbon from 1693 until his death at 80 years of age.²⁴ Dr Edmund Tanner, bishop of Cork, consecrated in Rome, stopped in Lisbon on his way home in 1575. He was accompanied by David Wolfe SJ, Robert Rochfort SJ, who had worked in Lisbon, and by Charles Lee SJ.

Maurice MacBrien (1567–86) of Emly returned, by way of Spain and Portugal, to his diocese in April 1574. He spent an unspecified length of time in Lisbon before reaching Ireland. He died in prison.²⁵ His contemporary, Maurice Fitzgibbon (MacGibbon), archbishop of Cashel, was in Oporto in 1565, and died there in or about 1678.²⁶ Hugh O'Reilly, archbishop of Armagh (1628–53), studied at the University of Coimbra in the years around 1605.²⁷

Coming to the end of the bishops in Lisbon it is notable that only one rector of the Irish college there became a bishop. This was Bartholomew Crotty, who was rector during the last years of the college (1799–1811); he was made bishop of Cloyne in 1833 and died in 1846.

The bishops educated in Lisbon were learned and distinguished men.²⁸ Most of them had studied at the universities of either Coimbra or Évora

---

22 He and his brother Matthew came to Portugal in 1604. He spent only six months in St Patrick's College, Lisbon, before going on to Salamanca and the University of Coimbra: O'Boyle, op. cit., p. 94. Mathew eventually 'married a wealthy, titled Spanish lady': O'Boyle, p. 95. **23** G. da C., p. 418. **24** G. da C., pp 28, 417–18; G. da C., pp 16–22. **25** G. da C., pp 33, 196, 416–7. **26** Ibid. p. 417. **27** Ibid. **28** Daniel O'Daly OP, might be termed a reluctant bishop. Born in Kerry in 1595, known as Frei Domingos do Rosario, he served his order, his religion, his country and his adopted country over many year as a priest and as a diplomat. He wrote a learned history of the Geraldine family and was entrusted over many years with special and delicate diplomatic missions. He was adviser to the king and confessor to the queen and wielded much influence at court. Founder of Corpo Santo and Bom Sucesso he was offered, and turned

and many wrote scholarly works. It has not been possible, within the limits of this work, to go into that side of their careers, but it is heartening to note that increasing interest is being shown in the lives of those churchmen who studied on the continent. This is not only true of the archdioceses of Armagh or Dublin but, happily, studies of our prelates in all dioceses are increasing in number and recognition is being given to these men who were Europeans in a real sense. A study of the priests and prelates who attended the Portuguese universities is long overdue.

down, several bishoprics, including Braga, Goa and, in the end, accepted Coimbra reluctantly, but died in 1662 or 1663, before being consecrated.

CHAPTER 5

The Students

The College of St Patrick in Lisbon was ushered into being in 1590 with twenty students, fleeing from Ireland, which at the time could offer them neither the possibility of a formal education nor the special training for a seminarian. Among the earliest students or 'subjects'[1] who enrolled were Stephen 'Polyhistor' White, Cornelius da Rocha (Carrick or McCarrick), Patrick Wall, James Everard, Pierce Archer (Bowman), Bartholomew Barr, Edward Clare, Bernard Connor, Dermot Hogan, Nicholas Leynach SJ, Anthony Lynch, Joseph Donelly OFM and Matthew Machra II. Some of the earliest ordinations of Irish clerics in Lisbon were carried out by Bishop Cornelius O'Mulryan (Ryan) OFM, of Killaloe, between 1587 and 1611. There were at least twenty-eight Irish seminarians ordained by the Irish prelate, and nine were given minor orders by him.[2]

During the centuries from foundation to closure the numbers attending the college fluctuated due to a variety of reasons. There were changes in conditions, in both Ireland and Portugal. The causes were common to all ages – political unrest, wars, travelling difficulties and natural disasters. The listing which follows gives student numbers, and boarders, in the college from 1590 to the 1830s.[3]

---

1 The word 'subject' is frequently used in correspondence between rectors. This is part of the special vocabulary used to disguise the 'clandestine commerce of a unique kind … written with possible interception in mind': see R.W. Richardson, op. cit., p. 112. Code-words were used by which the illegally travelling clerical students were introduced to the rector of an Irish college on the continent by the superior of the Jesuit mission in Ireland. Both the letter writer and recipient were always conscious of the fact that the letter could fall into the wrong hands. Other words were 'apprentice' or 'clerk' for a student, 'landlord' for a bishop, and 'factory' for a seminary. See Patrick J. Corish, *Arch. Hib.*, loc. cit., pp 85–103. **2** See Fenning, 1. Ordination lists by Hugh Fenning in *Collectanea Hibernica* (1989–90). I have to acknowledge with thanks Fr. Fenning's reading of this Chapter and Chapter 7, and his many helpful comments and suggestions. **3** A look at the brief chronology, which is included here gives events which may not be familiar to readers, as well as some other well-known happenings which are included as a link between both. See José

Year	Events	Number of collegians	Convictores[4]
1588	Spanish Armada		
1590		20	
1592		24	
1599	Plague in Lisbon		
1601	Battle of Kinsale		
1606		35	
1620		17	
1624		21	
1628		15	
1630	Dutch occupation of north east Brazil		
1633		12	
1638		12?	
1639		12	
1640	Restoration of Portuguese monarchy under Braganza dynasty		
1649		14	
1655		12	
1658		12	
1662	Catherine of Braganza marries Charles II on 21 May 1662, in London		
1665		9	2
	Plague in London		
1666	Fire of London		
1669		10	
1672		13	2
1675		13	
1681		13	3
1685		13	2
1690		11	
1693		11	
1699	First shipment of gold from Brazil to Lisbon		
1700		9	4

Saraiva, op. cit., pp 154–66. The list of clerical students numbers and boarders is compiled from data from a variety of sources already listed in Chapter 1. 4 *Convictores* were boarders, usually of school-going age, whose fees helped to defray the college expenses, since their official funds were almost always in arrears. They appear to have started to attend the college in the second half of the seventeenth century.

THE STUDENTS

Year	Events	Number of collegians	Convictores
1703	Methuen trade treaty between Portugal and Britain		
1705		10	4
1711		11	
1720		12	15
1726		9	
1729	Diamonds discovered in Bahia, Brazil		
1734		10	12
	Gold discovered in Mato Grosso, Brazil		
1742		10	19
1743		10	21
1745	Battle of Culloden	8	18 or 21
1749		7	23
1750	Pombal comes to power		
1754		8	20
1755		8	
	Earthquake in Lisbon; eruption of Mount Etna		
1759	Jesuits expelled from Portugal		
1782	American Independence		
1789	French Revolution		
1798	Rising in Ireland		
1800	Act of Union		
1801		12	
1803	Robert Emmet's rising		
1805	Battle of Trafalgar		
1807	Portugal invaded by French Royal family leave for Brazil		
1808	Start of Peninsular War		
1811	French retreat to Spanish frontier		
1813	French leave Portugal		
1815	Battle of Waterloo		
1822	Brazil independent		
1826	D. Pedro of Brazil, king of Portugal		
1834	Religious orders suppressed in Portugal		

THE IRISH COLLEGE AT LISBON

The Student Index, which follows, lists over five hundred names of collegians – some who were definitely students of St Patrick's College, Lisbon, others possibly students there, although no documentary evidence of this was found. The information regarding each student was obtained mainly from a variety of sources.[5] In the Index section of this chapter I have kept footnotes to a minimum because of the large number of entries. So. for each name I have listed several relevant references under one footnote.[6]

MATTHEW AMARAL SJ was given minor orders on 4 April 1616. The name is also given as Damarel. He was born *c*.1597 and entered the Society of Jesus in Évora in 1618. He has been identified as Matthew Gibbons.[7]

RAYMOND ANGLIS was ordained on 5 June 1618.[8]

EDWARD ANKES returned to Ireland some time between 1590 and 1615 as a secular.[9]

JAMES ARCHER was in the college from 1692 to 1695 and was ordained before 1692, when he started to celebrate Foundation masses.[10]

LUKE ARCHER, a secular priest, returned to Ireland some time between 1590 and 1615.[11]

---

5 The Irish Jesuit Archives, incl. the MacErlean Transcripts; Finegan's 'Biographical Dictionary'; Father Hugh Fenning's ordination lists 1587–1850, already cited; Goncalves da Costa's source-work, also previously cited; manuscript material in the Dublin Diocesan Archives; the Irish Dominican Archives. I have also found useful material in various libraries and archives in Lisbon, including the Biblioteca Nacional, Arquivo Nacional da Torre de Tombo (ANTT), Biblioteca da Ajuda, and Academia das Ciencias (BACL). There is some manuscript material on Irish subjects in the Ajuda Library at the Ajuda Palace, Belém. The printed works consulted will be found in the bibliography. Names of several priests will be found in *An Act for Registering the Popish Clergy 1703 with the Register of 1704* (Dublin, 1705) hereafter *Register, 1704* and in 'Index to the Priests of the Meath Diocese 1704–1993 by Rev. P. O'Connell, in Olive Curran (ed.), *History of the diocese of Meath, 1860–1993* (Mullingar, 1995), pp 1222–53 (hereafter *Meath List*). **6** The list covers the period from 1590 to the end of the eighteenth century. Because of the lack of college records after 1755 and the paucity of information on enrolments after 1778, I have included material on students of the college in the latter part of the eighteenth and early nineteenth centuries in Chapter 7, on the last years of the college. **7** LIS/7; G. da C., p. 419. **8** LIS/7. **9** G. da C., p. 409. **10** LIS/2. **11** G. da C., p. 409.

THE STUDENTS

PIERCE ARCHER was admitted to the college in 1592 against the rules in response to a request by the bishop of Ossory, Thomas Strong, so he was, possibly, from that diocese.[12]

RAPHAEL ARCHER (I) was ordained on 24 May 1698. He said, Masses for the intentions of the benefactor, Senhor Luís Fernandes de Almada, in the college chapel until he left for Ireland on 7 July 1699.[13]

RAPHAEL ARCHER (II) was ordained sub-deacon on 21 December 1700.[14]

NICHOLAS ARTHUR was ordained on 20 September 1642. Was he Father Nicholas Arthur from Limerick city, who sponsored candidates for Spanish knighthoods in some years between 1648 and 73?[15]

PATRICK AUSTIN was ordained on 5 October 1721.[16]

THOMAS AUSTIN was admitted to the college in 1685 with Roger Mathews. He was parish priest of St Nicholas's in Francis Street, Dublin, until his death in 1741.[17]

WILLIAM BARKER ordained on 18 June 1713, was still in the college in 1717.[18]

CORNELIUS BARNABY, a secular priest, returned to Ireland between 1590 and 1615.[19]

JOHN BARRON, born c.1584 in Clonmel, diocese of Waterford/Lismore, son of Gualfridum Barron and Beal White, he was in the Lisbon college from 1599, until he left for St Patrick's College, Salamanca, on 9 June 1603.[20]

PETER BARNWELL SJ, born on 10 October 1709 in Bremore, diocese of Dublin, entered the Jesuits in 1726, and returned to the Irish mission in 1741. Gonçalves da Costa gives his name as Patrick.[21]

BARTHOLOMEW BARR received tonsure on 23 September 1600. He was probably a student of the Irish College, Lisbon, and was son of Edward Barr and Catherine Chilla, native of Brida(?), Ireland (could this be Bredagh Cross, Drimoleague, Co. Cork?).[22]

---

12 Ibid. G. da C., p. 210. **13** Fenning, 2, p. 62; LIS/2; G. da C., p. 413. **14** Fenning, 2, p. 62. **15** Ibid., 1, p. 107; see M.K. Walsh, *Spanish knights of Irish origin*, i–iv (hereafter shortened to *Knights*) i, pp 22, 25, 27; 'iii, pp 3, 5, 17. **16** Fenning, 2, p. 62. **17** MT 1685: H. Fenning, in Kelly and Keogh (eds), op. cit., p. 189. **18** Fenning, 2, p. 62; LIS/4. **19** LIS/4. **20** D.J. O'Doherty, *Arch. Hib.* 2 (1913) 16. **21** LIS/4; G. da C., p. 419. **22** Fenning, 1, p. 107.

MICHAEL BARROS (BARRICK) SJ was born in (New) Ross, diocese of Ferns, in 1586, entered the Society of Jesus in 1606, aged eighteen years, studied in Évora and Coimbra and returned to Ireland in 1617, having been ordained in 1615 in Coimbra. He died in New Ross on 26 March 1648.[23]

ROBERT BATH, from County Meath, student of St Patrick's, entered the Jesuits in Rome in 1604.[24]

BERNO — See BYRNE.

BIRNO — See DA CRUZ.

ROBERT BLAKE ordained and returned to Ireland some time before 1615.[25]

MICHAEL BLUETT, ordained on 10 February 1709.[26]

GREGORY BODKIN SJ was born in city of Galway in 1590, son of Leo Bodkin and Isabel Lynch. He was in St Patrick's College from 1610 until his ordination on 21 June 1615. He entered the Jesuits in 1620 and he was proctor of the college in 1627.[27]

JOHN BOHELLY, ordained on 18 August 1709.[28]

NICHOLAS BRAY was in the college before 1592 and left for Valladolid in May 1592. He returned to Ireland in 1619.[29]

BRENNAN — See O'BRENNAN.

ALEXANDER BROWN was ordained on 28 August 1652.[30]

CHRISTOPHER BROWN received minor orders on 15 February 1704.[31]

DERMOT BROWN — See DERMOT BRYN.

EUSTACE BROWN, ordained on 24 September 1672, was from the diocese of Cashel and later became bishop of Killaloe (1713–24). He received a doctorate *cum laude* 31 December 1681 at the University of Évora.[32]

HENRY BROWN, died some time between 1590 and 1600.[33]

IGNATIUS BROWN SJ, diocese of Waterford/Lismore, received Minor Orders on 29 June 1679. He was born in 1661, entered the Jesuits in 1679

23 G. da C., p. 420; MT 1615.   **24** MT 1615.   **25** LIS/4.   **26** Fenning, 2, p. 62.   **27** Fenning, 1, p. 108; LIS/4 & 7.   **28** Fenning, 2, p. 62.   **29** G. da C., p. 400; MT Precis 6 July 1619.   **30** Fenning, 1, p. 108.   **31** Fenning, 2, p. 63.   **32** G. da C., p. 54; *Register, 1704*.   **33** LIS/4.

and studied in Coimbra. He returned to Kilkenny and after ten years there returned to Spain, where died two years later (in 1707).³⁴

JAMES BROWN SJ was in the college before 1705. He afterwards became rector of the Irish College, Salamanca (1705–8).³⁵

DERMOT BRYN (BROWN) was ordained before June 1624, when he signed a memorial with others, as Father Dermitius Bryn, protesting against the compulsion to attend lectures at a distance from the college and against the appointment of a Portuguese as rector of the college.³⁶

BRUNO — See BROWN.

FRANCIS BUI (BRAT) left for the Irish mission at some time between 1590 and 1615.³⁷

FRANCIS BURKE (DE BURGO): Gonçalves da Costa claims that this man was, *com certeza* (certainly), a student of the Irish College, Lisbon, and vicar-general of Tuam. He gives no dates, but equates him with the archbishop of Tuam (1714–23).³⁸

JOHN DE BURGO, was ordained on 23 May 1621, studied at the College of the Purification, University of Évora, 1622–5, where he was described as 'Mestre João de Burgos', a theologian in the college. He later became archbishop of Tuam (1647–67).³⁹

BURKE — See DE BURGO.

EDMUND BUTLER, ordained on 1 May 1616.⁴⁰

FRANCISCO BUTLER received minor orders on 14 September 1660.⁴¹

JAMES BUTLER SJ was in the college before 1615, when he joined the Jesuits. He returned to Ireland and was on the mission in 'Ross, East Munster in 1621'.⁴²

JOHN BUTLER SJ was ordained on 8 June 1755.⁴³

PETER BUTLER was in the college before 1615.⁴⁴

---

34 Fenning 2, p. 63; LIS/4; G. da C., p. 421. **35** O'Doherty, loc. cit., March 1874, p. 247; G. da C., p. 421. **36** G. da C., pp 260–2, 412; LIS/4. **37** LIS/4. **38** G. da C., p. 416. **39** LIS/4 & 7.; G. da C., p. 410. **40** LIS/7; G. da C., p. 410. **41** LIS/7. **42** G. da C., p. 421; LIS/4; MT Precis, 19 Nov. 1621; Finegan, op. cit., p. 20. **43** Fenning, 3, p. 144. **44** LIS/4.

THE IRISH COLLEGE AT LISBON

RICHARD BUTLER died some time before 1600.[45]

WILLIAM BUTLER died some time between 1590 and 1600.[46]

DENIS BYRNE was ordained on 17 March 1714.[47]

GEORGE BYRNE was ordained on 2 October 1718. He was later attached to St Catherine's, Meath Street, Dublin.[48]

GERALD BYRNE was examined for minor orders on 18 March 1641.[49]

ROBERT BYRNE SJ was from the diocese of Dublin. He entered the Jesuit Order in 1605. See also Robert da Cruz and Coutinho.[50]

NICHOLAS CADET died some time between 1590 and 1615.[51]

CORMAC CALLAGHAN, son of Cormac Caliano and Ursula Nigreli, was ordained on 24 June 1617.[52]

PATRICK CALLAGHAN SJ was a student in St Patrick's and was from diocese of Dublin. He was working there in 1733.[53]

MICHAEL CANTWELL SJ was a native of Tipperary, diocese of Cashel. He was born 1589, entered the Jesuits 1605 and was ordained before 1607. He was dismissed from the order. He is identified by MacErlean as Miguel de Morais, Michael Morales. He died in 1630.[54]

DANIEL CARBERY was ordained on 22 December 1646.[55]

NICHOLAS CARBERY was ordained on 24 January 1694 and said Foundation masses until he left for Ireland on 10 April 1697.[56]

CARLO DELLA MADRE DI DIO OFM was ordained before 1625, joined the Franciscans and was Guardian of the monastery of Xabregas in Lisbon. He was a Master of Theology. His name appears on a list compiled by G.B. Pallotto, collector in the Nunciature, Lisbon, and sent to Cardinal Bandini. It contained the names of eminent former collegians of St Patrick's worthy of elevation to vacant sees in Ireland. The list is dated 30 August 1625.[57]

DANIEL CARNE was in the college for some time before he departed for Valladolid in May 1592. He is identified by G. da Costa as Daniel O'Carroll, who had been vicar-general of the diocese of Killaloe for six years in 1605.[58]

---

45 Ibid.   **46** Ibid.   **47** Fenning, 2, p. 63.   **48** Ibid; LIS/4.   **49** G. da C., p. 411; LIS/7.   **50** G da C., op. cit., pp 409, 420; LIS/4.   **51** LIS/4.   **52** Fenning, 1, p. 108.   **53** LIS/4.   **54** G. da C., pp 421, 430; MT 1615.   **55** Fenning, 1, p. 108.   **56** Fenning, 2, p. 63; LIS/2, 4. Foundation masses were the obligatory masses offered for the foundation benefactors.   **57** LIS/4.   **58** Ibid. G. da C., pp 96 & 409.

[62]

THE STUDENTS

JAMES CARNE was ordained on 19 September 1609 in the cathedral, Lisbon by Bishop O'Mulryan. He was son of Mon.do (*sic*) and Joana Carne.[59]

JOHN CARPENTER, ordained on 18 June 1752, was later archbishop of Dublin (1770–86).[60]

MALACHY CARRANO was examined for orders on 4 July 1638. He was a student of the Colégio da Purificão, University of Évora, 1639–45.[61]

CARRICK – See DA ROCHA, CORNELIUS.

CHARLES CARROL, son of Daniel Carlho and Joanna Finea, diocese of Limerick, was ordained on 25 February 1680.[62]

CHARLES CARTHY, from the diocese of Limerick, took minor orders on 29 June 1671.[63]

DANIEL CARTHY was in the college *c.*1624 and signed the memorial of protest dated 1 June of that year.[64]

DENIS CARTHY this student was involved as leader of serious disturbances and disruptions in the college before 1629.[65]

DOMINIC – See DA SILVA, DOMINIC.

FLORENCE CARTHY was ordained on 4 July 1671 and left in 1676.[66]

LORENZO CARTHY was a secular priest who returned to Ireland at some time between 1590 and 1615.[67]

RICHARD CARY SJ from Waterford, was born in 1617, entered the Jesuits in 1639, was ordained on 1 October 1651, and died in 1696.[68]

THOMAS CASEY returned to Ireland some time between 1590 and 1615 as a secular priest.[69]

HUGO CASTELLO died some time between 1590 and 1615.[70]

CHIRROVAO – See KIRWAN.

---

59 Fenning, 1, p. 108; LIS/4. **60** Fenning, 3, p. 144. **61** LIS/7; G. da C., op. cit., p. 411. **62** Fenning, 2, p. 64. **63** Ibid. **64** G da C., op. cit., p. 262; LIS/4; see Dermot Bryn (Brown) above. **65** See Chapter 6 for details of disturbances. **66** Fenning, 2, p. 64. **67** LIS/4. **68** Fenning, 1, p. 108. **69** LIS/4. **70** Ibid.

EDWARD CLARE (CLERY) SJ, born Waterford in May 1580, was ordained in 1604. He attended St Patrick's College and in 1604 entered the Society of Jesus. He returned to Ireland in 1614 and was based in the city of Cork in 1621.[71]

WILLIAM CLARKE was ordained on 16 May 1751.[72]

CLERY – See CLARE.

JOHN CLINCH, started first-year Philosophy at the Irish College in 1704 and was ordained on 18 August 1709. He was vicar-general of Dublin in 1735.[73]

LAURENCE CLINE was ordained on 13 June 1732.[74]

JAMES CLINTON ordained before 1685, was in St Patrick's from 1685 to 1691.[75]

PATRICK CLINTON died some time between 1590 and 1600.[76]

CORNELIUS CLUNE was ordained on 19 October 1800.[77]

EDMOND CODY, from diocese of Ossory, was ordained on 22 April 1804 and became parish priest of Kilnacow in 1808.[78]

RICHARD CODY was ordained on 8 April 1618.[79]

HUGH COLAN (CULLEN) SJ received minor orders on 18 December 1648. He was born in County Westmeath on 17 January 1627 and joined the Jesuits in 1648. He was involved in the affairs of James II, on whose behalf he returned to Lisbon in 1690 as Ambassador Extraordinary, and had also been chaplain at London to Queen Catherine (of Braganza), the Portuguese wife of Charles II.[80]

PHILIP COLMAN, son of Francis Colman and Margaret Terelea, was ordained on 26 December 1675. In 1704 he was registered in Nenagh, diocese of Cashel, as parish priest of Ardmayle, Ballysheehan and Erry, and lived at Gortmakellis, aged 53 years.[81]

---

71 LIS/4, 6; G. da C., p. 422; MT Precis, 19 Nov. 1621 & 8 April 1615; Finegan, 'Biographical Dictionary', p. 27.   **72** Fenning, 3, p. 145.   **73** Fenning, 2, p. 64; LIS/3 & 4.   **74** Fenning, 2, p. 64.   **75** LIS/4; MT 18 Mar. 1690.   **76** LIS/2, 4.   **77** Fenning, 3, p. 145.   **78** Ibid.   **79** LIS/7.   **80** Fenning, 1, p. 108; G. da C., p. 422; MT 23 June 1690.   **81** Fenning, 2, p. 64; *Register*, 1704.

CORNELIUS COMEE was ordained before 1682. He celebrated Foundation Masses in the college from 1682 to 1685.[82]

HENRY COMERFORD, possibly from the diocese of Ossory, was ordained on 17 January 1658. He appears as a sponsor for a candidate for a Spanish knighthood in 1665, and hailed from Castlekelly, County Kilkenny.[83]

JAMES COMERFORD (I) was ordained on 11 January 1705.[84]

JAMES COMERFORD (II), son of Nicholas Comforte and Mariana Corea, born in Oporto, was ordained on 9 August 1656.[85]

PATRICK COMERFORD OSA, from Waterford, lifelong friend and schoolmate of Luke Wadding, studied in the Irish College. Lisbon, in France and in the University of Coimbra. He was bishop of Waterford, 1629–52.[86]

THOMAS COMERFORD was ordained on 9 May 1628.[87]

LUDOVICH CONEGAN died some time between 1590 and 1615.[88]

WILLIAM CONICH was ordained on 8 September 1793.[89]

PATRICK CONNELL received Minor Orders on 29 June 1671.[90]

BERNARD CONNOR, son of John and Honoria, from diocese of Ardfert, was ordained on 4 June 1594.[91]

WILLIAM CONNOR, son of John Conor and Honora Nibrii, was from the diocese of Emly and was ordained on 18 December 1649. He studied theology at Évora.[92]

CONNOR – See also O'CONNOR.

RICHARD CONWAY SJ studied Humanities in St Patrick's before he entered the Jesuits in Coimbra on 22 July 1592. He may be Richard Connye, who took part with Patrick Sinnott in a dialogue in verse, at the official opening of the Irish College on Whit Sunday, May 1592, which was described in a letter in the Lansdowne Papers.[93]

---

82 LIS/2, 4.   **83** Fenning, 1, p. 108; *Knights*, iii, p. 4.   **84** Fenning, 2, p. 64.
85 Fenning, 1, p. 108.   **86** LIS/4; O'Boyle, op. cit., pp 183–4; G. da C., p. 415.
87 LIS/7.   **88** LIS/4.   **89** Fenning, 3, p. 145.   **90** Fenning, 2, p. 64.
91 Fenning, 1, p. 108. This is the only Lisbon student whose name I have found from the old diocese of Ardfert.   **92** Fenning, 1 pp 108–9.   **93** G. da C., pp 203, 247 & 408.

CORBERY – See CARBURY.

JOHN CORKERAN born c.1668, ordained 1693, was from the diocese of Dublin. He said Foundation masses from 1692 to 1697. He left for Ireland on 1 March 1697; was registered as parish priest Cloniske (where he lived), Balrothery and Balscaddon.[94]

BARNABY CORNELIO returned to Ireland some time between 1590 and 1615.[95]

DERMOT CORNELIO OFM, son of Dermot Cornelio and Grania Sa, Derry, was given minor orders by Bishop O'Mulryan in the cathedral, Lisbon, on 23 September 1600.[96]

WILLIAM COSGRAVE took minor orders on 19 September 1664.[97]

ROBERT COUTINHO SJ – See Roberto da Cruz and Robert Byrne.

STEPHEN CREAGH died some time between 1590 and 1600.[98]

CRAGH – See MAGRATH.

CREDA – See RIORDAN.

CREVAEOUS – See MAGRATH.

JOHN CROFTON said Foundation masses for Jerónimo Ximenes from 1684 to 1688.[99]

BARTHOLOMEW CROTTY was rector from 1799 to 1811 and bishop of Cloyne and Ross 1833–46.[100]

WILLIAM CROTTY was ordained on 9 March 1805.[101]

CRUZ – See also MAGRATH.

JOHN DA CRUZ SJ, born in Dublin in 1603, was a collegian in St Patrick's before joining the Jesuits in 1620. Later studied at Évora.[102]

ROBERT DA CRUZ SJ was born in Dublin in 1584 or 1589; possibly a student in St Patrick's; joined the Jesuits in 1604, studied philosophy, theology, Greek and Hebrew in Coimbra. Although the names Robert Coutinho, Robert Byrne and Roberto da Cruz are often listed as separate,

94 LIS/2, 4; Register; 1704.   **95** LIS/2, 4.   **96** Fenning, 1. p. 109; LIS/4.
97 Fenning, 2, p. 65.   **98** LIS/4.   **99** Ibid. 2, 4.   **100** See Chapters 3, 4, 7.
101 Fenning, 3, p. 145.   **102** G. da C., p. 424.

it would appear that they all refer to one person. Other variations of the names are Coyler and Birne.[103]

CRUZ, WILLIAM DA – See MAGRATH.

CRUZ, ROQUE DA – See MCGEOGHEGAN.

CULLEN, HENRY SJ – See COLAN.

WILLIAM CULLEN said Foundation masses in the college, 1685–8. A Father William Cullen was appointed parish priest in Castlepollard, Mullingar, County Westmeath, around the year 1704.[104]

DENIS CULLENAN said Foundation masses in the college, 1679–82.[105]

JAMES CUSACK, ordained in 1692, said Foundation masses until 1694, when he left for Évora, where he graduated as *licenciado*.[106]

JOHN CUSACK (QUISACO) SJ was a student at St Patrick's before he entered the Jesuits in Rome on 28 October 1606.[107]

RICHARD DALTON was ordained on 30 September 1644.[108]

DALMATIUS DALY, son of Maurice Daleo and Margaret Giban, of Brosnahe (*sic*), was ordained on 8 April 1618.[109]

DANIEL DALY, son of Charles Daly and Mary Keeffe, was given minor orders on 1 April 1685.[110]

DIDACUS (JAMES) DALY, studied Rhetoric in St Patrick's, ordained on 11 January 1711, received the degree of *licenciado* on 8 May 1712, in the University of Évora.[111]

JOHN DALY was ordained on 30 September 1644.[112]

MICHAEL DALY, a collegian in 1755 when the earthquake struck Lisbon, later became rector (1782–98).[113]

DAMARAL – See AMARAL.

BARNABY DANIEL SJ, a student at St Patrick's who entered the Jesuits in 1609.[114]

103 Ibid.; LIS/4; MT 1621. **104** LIS/4; *Meath List*, p. 1229. **105** LIS/2, 4. **106** Ibid.; G. da C., p. 414. **107** G. da C., pp 409, 431; MT 1615. **108** Fenning, 1, p. 109. **109** Ibid. **110** Fenning, 2, p. 65. **111** Ibid; G. da C. p. 414. **112** Fenning, 1, p. 109. **113** See also Chapter 6 for detail of Father Daly. **114** G. da C., pp 409 & 424; MT 1615.

RICHARD DANIEL SJ, a student of St Patrick's, whose name is also given as R. David, son of Dermot Daniel and Margaret Keating, Lismore diocese, was a student of the college, ordained on 27 March 1621.

NICHOLAS DAY was ordained before 1627.[116]

CHARLES DEALE, ordained in 1678, lived in Ballentullagh, County Westmeath, in 1704, aged 60.[117]

JOSEPH JOY DEANE, from the diocese of Dublin, lived in St Patrick's in March 1807, as a member of staff.[118]

DE HONOCHO, DE NOCHO – See DONOGHUE.

EDMUND DEIS was ordained on 5 November 1633.[119]

NICHOLAS DEISE, ordained on 28 September 1627, signed the 1624 memorial already mentioned.[120]

BARTHOLOMEW DELEHID died some time between 1590 and 1600.[121]

BERNARD DELANY was ordained on 9 June 1827.[122]

CHARLES DEMPSEY SJ, ordained on 22 March 1699, was registered in 1704 as parish priest of St Bride's, Bride Street, Dublin, aged 28 years. He said Foundation masses from July 1699 to 1701.[123]

JAMES DESERE, given minor orders on 12 June 1615, was son of John and Juliana Lynch, Galway.[124]

ANTHONY DEVEREUX was ordained on 8 July 1657.[125]

WILLIAM DEVEREUX who returned to the mission before 1615, was vicar-general of the diocese of Ferns.[126]

JOHN DEVLIN was a subscriber to *The lives of the saints* by Alban Butler, published in Dublin in 1802. His address was given as St Patrick's, Lisbon; whether he was then a student or on the staff does not appear.[127]

---

115 Fenning, 17, p. 109; LIS/4, 7; MT 25 Mar. 1621.   116 LIS/7.   117 *Register, 1704*.   118 DDA, letter from Deane to Troy, 14 March 1807.   119 LIS/7.   120 G. da C., op. cit., pp 262 & 411. See Dermot Bryn (Brown) above.   121 LIS/4.   122 Fenning, 3, p. 146.   123 Fenning, 2, p. 65; *Register, 1704*; G. da C. p. 413; LIS/2, 4; MT 11 & 13 April 1695.   124 Fenning, 1, p. 109.   125 Ibid.   126 LIS/4; G. da C., p. 416.   127 This information was kindly given to me by Father Hugh Fenning, OP.

PETER DILLON (I) was ordained on 10 August 1682. He was appointed parish priest of Stamullan, County Meath, in 1690 and was aged 45 years in 1704.[128]

PETER DILLON (II) received minor orders on 21 September 1708.[129]

THOMAS DIVINEY was given minor orders on 7 September 1721.[130]

PATRICK DOBIN was ordained c.5 June 1615 and switched to Salamanca in January 1616. According to his 'oath', dated 26 January, he was from Thomastown, County Kildare, son of John Dobbin and Margaret Langton, and was 23 years old.[131]

DOBBYN – See DUBIN.

DONATUS was ordained on 18 May 1589. He was son of Philip and Mary, diocese of Limerick.[132]

PATRICK DONNELLAN, a priest mentioned as being 'alive yet' by Fr Daly in 1787.[133]

ROBERT DONOGHUE, son of William Donoghue and Catherine Mooney, was ordained on 31 December 1606.[134]

DAVID DOURAN was given minor orders on 21 September 1623.[135]

JOHN DOURMOUR died some time between 1590 and 1600.[136]

BARNABY DOURNOUX OFM was a student at St Patrick's before he joined the Franciscans and returned to Ireland between 1590 and 1615.[137]

ANDREW DOWDALL was ordained on 8 March 1704.[138]

MICHAEL DOWDALL said Foundation masses from 1684 to 19 February 1685, when he left for Ireland.[139]

PATRICK DOWDALL received minor orders on 6 June 1688. He lived at Arthurstown, parish of Charlestown, Clonkeene, Philipstown, Tallanstown (Dundalk) and Clonkeegan, County Louth, in 1704.[140]

128 Fenning, 2, p. 65; *Meath List*, p. 1231; *Register, 1704*. **129** Fenning, 2. **130** Ibid. **131** LIS/4; G. da C., op. cit., p. 411; O'Doherty, *Arch. Hib.*, 2 (1913), 34. **132** Fenning, 1, p. 109. **133** DDA, letter, Daly to Troy, 20 May 1787; may have been a visiting Dominican father who was then based in London. **134** Fenning, 1, p. 109. **135** LIS/4, 7. **136** LIS/4. **137** Ibid. **138** Fenning, 2, pp 65–6. **139** LIS/4. **140** Fenning, 2, p. 66; *Register, 1704*, which gives date of

PETER DOWDALL (I) was ordained on 20 October 1675 and said Foundation Masses from 1675 to 1679.[141]

PETER DOWDALL (II) was ordained in Lisbon. In 1704 he was aged 51, and was attached to the parishes of Ardee, Kildenock, Smaremor, Maperstown, Shanliss, Kilpatrick and Charlestown, County Louth.[142]

RICHARD DOWDALL SJ was working in Dublin in 1733 and had been a student in St Patrick's.[143]

THOMAS DOWDALL returned to Ireland some time between 1590 and 1615.[144]

WALTER DOWDALL was ordained before 1681.[145]

WILLIAM DOWDALL was ordained before 1679 and celebrated Foundation masses in the college until 1684.[146]

EDMUND THOMAS DOYLE was ordained on 22 September 1804 as Thomas.[147]

NICHOLAS DUBIN (DOBBIN) was described by the rector, Walter French, in 1592 as 'one of the best and most virtuous of the college'. This was in a letter to William Nogell (Nagle), a cousin of Nicholas.[148]

EUGENIO DUFFY went back to Ireland some time before 1615.[149]

NELANUS DUFFY (I) was a student of second-year Philosophy in the college, 1705–6.[150]

NELANUS DUFFY (II) OFM became a Franciscan and went back to Ireland some time between 1590 and 1616.[151]

PATRICK DUFFY returned to Ireland before 1616.[152]

JOHN BAPTIST DUGGAN SJ rector, born 1584, was from either the diocese of Ossory, or Killaloe. He studied Philosophy at St Patrick's and was a student at the University of Évora; entered the Jesuits in 1603, returned to Ireland and ministered in Galway. He was a close friend of Francis Kirwan, later bishop of Killala (1645–61). He died in Galway in 1642.[153]

---

ordination as 1691. **141** Fenning, 2; LIS/2, 4. **142** *Register*, 1704; possibly the same as Peter Dowdall (1). **143** LIS/4. **144** Ibid. **145** Ibid. **146** Ibid. **147** Fenning, 3, p. 146. **148** LIS/4; G. da C., p. 409. **149** LIS/4. **150** Ibid.; G. da C., p. 364. **151** G. da C., p. 407. **152** Ibid. p. 409. **153** Finegan, 'Biographical Dictionary', p. 49; MT 1615.

THE STUDENTS

JOHN DUNGAN was ordained on 22 December 1646.[154]

JOHN DUNN, from Dublin, was the first collegian sent by Archbishop Carpenter to Lisbon after the recovery of the college. Having finished his studies in the college, he stayed on to supervise the Philosophy course; he was rector from 1811 until 1823. He was appointed parish priest of Clondalkin in 1820, but did not return there until three years later.[155]

DUYER – See DWYER.

DONATO DWYER was in the seminary in June 1615.[156]

EDMOND – See REDMOND.

MICHAEL EGAN, ordained on 13 June 1829, was a native of Clara, County Meath and was appointed curate in Moyvore in 1846. He died in 1849.[157]

EDMUND ENNIS SJ, from Fethard, County Tipperary, was ordained on 21 September 1623, studied at Coimbra University and taught at the college of São Miguel, in the Azores in 1632. He held the chair of Theology in the Irish College in 1636.[158]

ALEXANDER EUSTACE was examined for Orders on 15 March 1641.[159]

ROBERT EUSTACE OFM was ordained on 30 November 1602. Son of Thomas Eustace and Joanna Power, he became a Franciscan and was companion to Father Luke Wadding. Returned to Ireland some time before 1615.[160]

CHARLES EVERARD received minor orders on 18 March 1641.[161]

CHRISTOPHER EVERARD went back to Ireland some time between 1590 and 1615.[162]

EDMUND EVERARD was ordained on 23 November 1681. In 1704, aged 45, he was living in the city of Waterford, parish of St Patrick.[163]

JAMES EVERARD SJ, from diocese of Cashel, studied Humanities in the Irish College. Born 1578, son of Redmond Everard, from Fethard, County

---

154 Fenning, 1, p. 110.   **155** DDA, letters, Daly to Troy and Dunn to Troy, 22 July 1791 and 9 August 1822. See also Chapter 7.   **156** LIS/4.   **157** Fenning, 3, p. 146; *Meath List*, p. 1232.   **158** LIS/4; G. da C., p. 425.   **159** LIS/7.   **160** Fenning, 1, p. 110; G. da C., p. 407.   **161** LIS/7.   **162** LIS/4.   **163** Fenning, 2, p. 66;

Tipperary, he entered the Society in 1598 and was ordained in 1604. Lectured on philosophy in the Irish College for some years before being recalled to Ireland in 1608; he spent some time in Dublin, Drogheda and Cashel and died in 1646. He was a brother of Sir John Everard, of the British House of Commons.[164]

ANDREW FALLON was ordained sub-deacon on 18 September 1649.[165]

DR JAMES FALLON, from the diocese of Clonfert, was ordained 21 July 1615. He was a son of Charles and Margaret Kelly. (O'Fallon, Fallon, O'Phelan are variations of the name found.) He was vicar-general of Clonfert, 1631–62, and was proposed by Rinuccini in 1645 as bishop of Achonry.[166]

DIDACUS FALLON was a notable preacher c.1625.[167]

ANDREW FARRELL SJ, from Ardagh diocese, was a native of Pallas, County Longford, and was 21 years old in 1614. He served in various offices in the college.[168]

RICHARD FARRELL (I) was ordained before 1699 and said Foundation masses in the college until 1706.[169]

RICHARD FARRELL (or Fotrel?)(II) was ordained before 1627.[170]

FERRAR, FERREIRA — See SMITH.

WILLIAM FINEO, son of Cornelius Fineo and Johanna MacNamara, was ordained on 31 December 1658.[171]

FITZANTHONY — See LYNCH, THOMAS.

JOHN FITZGERALD, from Dublin, ordained in 1684 and was registered in 1704 as aged 44 years and living in Church Street, the parish of Ballyfarmaul (sic).[172]

NICHOLAS FITZGERALD (I) was ordained on 2 May 1654.[173]

NICHOLAS FITZGERALD (II) was ordained on 14 August 1679.[174]

FITZHENRY — See HENRIQUES.

Register, 1704.   **164** Finegan, 'Biographical Dictionary', p. 52.   **165** Fenning, 1, p. 110.   **166** Ibid. G. da C., p. 296; LIS.4,7.   **167** LIS/4, he is probably the same as Dr James Fallon, above.   **168** Ibid. 6.   **169** LIS/2, 4 & 7.   **170** LIS/7.   **171** Fenning, 1, p. 110.   **172** *Register, 1704*.   **173** Fenning, 1, p. 110.   **174** Fenning,

THE STUDENTS

FITZTHOMAS, PHILIP – See HENRIQUES.

PETER FLANAGAN was ordained on 8 July 1657.[175]

RODRIGO FLANAGAN was ordained before 1679.[176]

TERENCE FLOOD received minor orders on 6 June 1688.[177]

ROBERT FORESTAL, son of Gerald Forostaly and Dorothy Kennedy, was ordained on 29 September 1676.[178]

RICHARD FOTTRIL (maybe the same as Richard Farrell, II above) was in the college around 1624.[179]

ROBERT FRENCH died between 1590 and 1600.[180]

JOHN FURLONG (I) received minor orders on 19 December 1738.[181]

JOHN FURLONG (II) was ordained on 21 December 1740.[182]

DERMOT FYAN was ordained on 11 June 1652.[183]

PATRICK GALVE was from Cork city, a son of Patricio Galve and Margaret de Rocha; he was ordained on 27 March 1621.[184]

WALTER GALE was ordained on 23 June 1619.[185]

DAVID GALLWEY SJ, from Cork; studied for a while in the Irish College, Lisbon, admitted to the Jesuits in Rome in 1604, aged 25 years, and returned to Ireland in 1608; ordained before 1604.[186]

JAMES GARLAND was ordained on 5 June 1615.[187]

JEROME GARVAN, ordained on 7 November 1734, born of Irish parents in the Azores, on the island of Fayal, diocese of Angra.[188]

ANDREW GAUGHRAN, from the diocese of Kilmore, was ordained on 4 March 1651.[189]

WILLIAM GEOGHEGAN, who left Dublin in 1686 for studies at Lisbon and Évora, returned to Dublin with testimonials in 1699.[190]

2, p. 66. **175** Fenning, 1, p. 110. **176** LIS/4, 7. **177** Fenning, 2, p. 67. **178** Ibid. **179** LIS/4; G. da C., p. 262. **180** LIS/4. **181** Fenning, 2, p. 67. **182** Fenning, 3, p. 147; probably the same as John Furlong (I) above. **183** Fenning, 1, p. 110. **184** LIS/4 & 7. **185** G. da C., p. 410. **186** Ibid. p. 425; MT 1615. **187** LIS/4. **188** Fenning, 2, p. 67. **189** Ibid. (1), p. 110. **190** This reference is also from Father Fenning – APF.SC. Irlanda 6, ff 555–6.

WILLIAM GEROD died some time between 1590 and 1615.[191]

GIBBONS – See AMARAL.

JAMES GIBBONS SJ, from Dublin, born in 1659, received minor orders on 18 August 1676, entered the Jesuits in 1677. He was ordained priest in 1691 in Coimbra. He lived in Grangegorman in 1704, aged 44 years and was parish priest of Kinsealy.[192]

NICHOLAS GIBBONS was ordained on 19 March 1717.[193]

JAMES GILL OFM returned to Ireland some time between 1590 and 1615.[194]

JOHN GLINCH was in second-year Philosophy in the college in 1706.[195]

GOULD – See GULD.

JOHN GRACE was ordained on 7 October 1753.[196]

MICHAEL GREAHAMES, ordained before 1689, was in the college from 1688 until 1692.[197]

EUGENE GRIFFIN returned to Ireland some time between 1590 and 1615.[198]

JAMES GRIFFIN, son of Matthew and Honora Mohona, native of Balifada, diocese of Killaloe, was ordained on 18 December 1599.[199]

LAURENCE GUBBINS received minor orders on 20 December 1697.[200]

SEBASTIAN GUIAM was ordained before 1699.[201]

JAMES GUINAN (also found as Genna), son of Richard Geinan and Alsona Doran of the city of Kilkenny, diocese of Ossory, was ordained on 27 May 1621.[202]

GEORGE GOULD, ordained before 1705, was in second-year Philosophy in the college in 1706.[203]

EDMUND HABERINO, ordained on 16 March 1669, said Foundation Masses in the college, 1670–6.[204]

---

191 LIS.4.   **192** Ibid.; Fenning, 2, p. 67; *Register, 1704*; *Reportorium Novum*. 2, 2 (1959/60), p. 264.   **193** Fenning, 2.   **194** LIS/4.   **195** G. da C., p. 364.   **196** Fenning, 3, p 148.   **197** LIS/2 & 4.   **198** LIS/4.   **199** Fenning, 1, p. 111.   **200** Fenning, 1, p. 68.   **201** G. da C., p. 413.   **202** Fenning, 1, pp 110–11; LIS/7.   **203** G. da C., p. 364; LIS/2, 4.   **204** Fenning, 2, p. 68; LIS/4; G. da C., p. 413.

JAMES HACKETT, ordained on 1 May 1715, was a student at the English College of Sts Peter and Paul, Lisbon.[205]

MICHAEL HACKETT, ordained in 1627 signed the letter of complaint in 1624; he attended the University of Évora from 1628 until 1635.[206]

NICHOLAS HACKETT died some time between 1590 and 1615.[207]

PATRICK HACKETT was ordained after 28 September 1629. His Portuguese was considered sufficient for permission to be granted him to hear confessions.[208]

PATRICK HAGAN, from the diocese of Clogher, was ordained on 21 December 1793. He was curate in Dundalk; taught Divinity at Lisbon; had been a scholar of Dr Crotty's and had some disagreement with him in 1804. He was said to have a violent temper. His name appears as a subscriber to Alban Butler's *The lives of the saints*, 3rd ed., Dublin, 1802. He died on 11 April 1818. Also appears as O'Hagan.[209]

THADDEUS HAGAN was ordained on 2 March 1755.[210]

PETER HAMELL was ordained on 20 October 1883.[211]

PATRICK HAMPTON was ordained on 2 July 1619.[212]

BARTHOLOMEW HANLON was ordained on 12 August 1736.[213]

PATRICK HANLON returned to Ireland some time between 1590 and 1615.[214]

THOMAS HARRIGAN was ordained deacon on 16 December 1650.[215]

HARRISON – Could be HENRIQUES.

WILLIAM HARTIGAN, from the diocese of Emly, ordained on 14 July 1622, was the son of Dermot Hardegano and Finola Marinha from the town of Cahergindes (*sic*).[216]

---

205 Fenning, 2.   **206** LIS/4 & 7; see Dermot Bryn (Brown) above; G. da C., p. 262, 411.   **207** LIS/4.   **208** LIS/7.   **209** Fenning, 3, p. 148; DDA, letter, Crotty to Troy 18 Aug. 1804; information regarding subscribers to Butler's *Lives of the saints* was kindly supplied by Father Hugh Fenning.   **210** Fenning, 3, p. 148.   **211** Ibid.   **212** LIS/7. The name Patrick Hamlius appears in the Irish Jesuit Archives, MT 25 Sept. 1598, which is possibly the same as Patrick Hampton, he is recorded as 'once a pupil in this seminary'.   **213** Fenning, 2, p. 68.   **214** LIS/4.   **215** Fenning, 1, p. 111.   **216** Ibid.

JAMES HARTY, from the archdiocese of Cashel, was ordained on 2 April 1650.[217]

HAY — See O'CONNOR HAY, PATRICK.

JAMES HAY, son of Thaddeus Hea and Silena Chakcau of the parish of Chilcheran (Kilkerrin), was ordained on 20 October 1675.[218]

JAMES HEELAN was ordained on 14 February 1663.[219]

MAURICE HEELAN was ordained on 18 October 1609.[220]

THOMAS HEELAN OSA, ordained on 2 September 1618, he was a son of John Hilano and Anna Flangolie, native of Doliscoren, Ireland, and was in St Patrick's before joining the Augustinians.[221]

HELANO, HILANO, HILAN, HYLENO — See HEELAN.

DENIS HELLGHANAN returned to Ireland sometime between 1590 and 1615.[222]

JOHN HENAN (HENANO) was ordained deacon on 2 September 1618.[223]

EDMUND HENNESSY was ordained on 11 March 1623.[224]

MICHAEL HENRIQUES (I) was ordained on 15 October 1679.[225]

MICHAEL HENRIQUES (II), son of Robert Henriques and Ilena de Sueton, was ordained on 19 March 1685.[226]

RICHARD HENRIQUES, from the diocese of Ferns, became sub-deacon on 18 December 1599; son of John Anriquez and Caterina Renet. He left Lisbon for Valladolid in May 1592 and is listed as one of those who left for Ireland some time before 1615.[227]

WILLIAM HENRIQUES, ordained before 1698, said Foundation masses from 1698 to 1705.[228]

JAMES HICKEY was ordained on 18 July 1751.[229]

---

217 Ibid. **218** Fenning, 2, p. 68. He could be either of two thus named in Co. Galway, one near Ballinasloe and the other in Connemara. **219** Ibid. **220** Fenning, 1, p. 111. **221** Ibid. **222** LIS/4. **223** Fenning, 1, p. 111. **224** LIS/7. **225** Fenning, 2, p. 68. **226** Fenning, 2, Register, 1704. **227** Fenning, 1, p. 111; LIS/4. **228** LIS/2, 4, 6. **229** Fenning, 3, p. 149.

EDMUND HIGGINS was given minor orders on 6 March 1700; he was involved in a disturbance in the college in 1705, when he was aged 24 years.[230]

JOHN HIGGINS SJ was a student at St Patrick's for a year before he joined the Jesuits in 1681; born in Waterford on 26 April, 1656, and was ordained in 1689. He was registered in Waterford city in 1704, in the parish of St Olaf (Olave). He was critical of the Portuguese management of the Irish college in a letter dated 30 November 1694. Died in 1733.[231]

CHARLES HOGAN, son of Hugh Hogan and Joanna Haya, from the diocese of Killaloe, received minor orders on 1 October 1606.[232]

DERMOT HOGAN OFM, son of Hugh and Ranalda and from the diocese of Killaloe, was given minor orders on 20 May 1595; he became a Franciscan and died on the way home to Ireland some time between 1595 and 1615.[233]

THADDEUS HOGAN died some time between 1590 and 1615.[234]

MATHEW HOLIWOOD received minor orders on 28 August 1618.[235]

DANIEL HORAN, from the diocese of Dublin, ordained by Dr Carpenter in 1785, left for Ireland in 1791, when he finished his course. He asked to remain in the college for some more time to review his Moral Theology. He died in 1794.[236]

ANDREW HORE was ordained on 25 August 1618.[237]

EDMUND HORE received minor orders in 1623; he signed the 1624 memorial.[238]

IGNATIUS HORE was ordained on 2 May 1654.[239]

THOMAS EDMUND HORE was ordained on 12 September 1658.[240]

THOMAS HOWLING died some time between 1590 and 1615.[241]

---

230 Ibid. (2), p. 68; LIS/4, 6; see Chapter 6.   **231** LIS/4; *Register, 1704*, the parish of St Olaf was a medieval parish in the city of Waterford.   **232** Fenning, 1, p. 111; LIS/4.   **233** Ibid.   **234** LIS/4.   **235** LIS/7.   **236** DDA, letter Daly to Troy, 22 July 1791; M.J. Curran, *Reportorium Novum*, i, 2 (1956), p. 488–90.   **237** G. da C., p. 410.   **238** LIS/4, 7; see Dermot Bryn (Brown) above.   **239** Fenning, 1, p. 112.   **240** Ibid.   **241** LIS/4.

DANIEL HURLEY, ordained on 2 July 1619, signed letter of complaint in 1624 sent to General of the Order in Rome.[242]

PATRICK HURLEY, from Cork, was ordained on 3 February 1728.[243]

WILLIAM HURLEY SJ, from Kilmallock, received minor orders on 21 September 1623.[244]

MICHAEL HURRANE OFM, studied at St Patrick's for a short time, became a Franciscan and left for the mission in Ireland between 1580 and 1615.[245]

IGNATIO – See NASH.

RAYMUND INGLIS was ordained on 4 January 1618.[246]

JOHN INKES died some time between 1590 and 1615.[247]

JOHN JENNET was a student from Dublin who came to St Patrick's from the Irish College, Lille, and left after six months on 21 July 1790, as he did not wish to take the 'oath'.[248]

PHILIP JONAS died some time between 1590 and 1615.[249]

NICHOLAS JONES, living in Donabate, County Dublin, in 1704, aged 36; was ordained in 1694 in Lisbon.[250]

PETER JOYCE received minor orders on 25 January 1709.[251]

REV. MR JOYCE, from the archdiocese of Tuam: presumably Hyacinth Joyce, who became rector in 1823. Cited in a letter from rector John Dunn to Archbishop Troy as willing to take over the Irish College, Lisbon, as rector in 1822. He had gone to Brazil in 1807, with the concurrence of the rector, Bartholomew Crotty, in the suite of a nobleman, who accompanied the royal family into exile during the French invasion. Returned in 1822 and took up residence at the college. Reputed to have been very influential at the court.[252]

WALTER JOYCE was ordained on 5 October 1721.[253]

---

[242] Fenning, 1, p. 112; see Dermot Bryn (Brown) above. [243] LIS/4; G. da C., p. 262. [244] LIS/7; MT 28 Apr. 1635. [245] LIS/4. [246] Fenning, 1, p. 112. [247] LIS/4. [248] DDA, letter, Daly to Troy, 21 July 1790. [249] LIS/4. [250] *Register, 1704*. [251] Fenning, 2, p. 69. [252] DDA letter, from John Dunn to Troy, 9 Aug. 1822. [253] Fenning, 2, p. 69.

THE STUDENTS

BARTHOLOMEW KEAN, ordained before 1698, said Foundation masses for a period from 1698 to 1705.[254]

DANIEL KEARNEY (I) was ordained on 25 March 1730.[255]

DANIEL KEARNEY (II), from the archdiocese of Cashel, took Minor Orders on 25 March 1621; he became vicar-general of Cashel.[256]

JOHN KEARNEY was ordained on 15 November 1629.[257]

THOMAS KEARNEY, from the diocese of Meath c.1801.[258]

NICHOLAS KEARNS – See Chapter 7.

JOHN KEATING (I) was given minor orders on 16 March 1696.[259]

JOHN KEATING (II) was ordained on 10 August 1736.[260]

ZEPHERINO KEATING was ordained on 22 May 1807.[261]

JOHN KEENAN, ordained on 12 June 1615, was son of William Quinao and Alisona of Bolani (*sic*) in Ireland. He studied in the Colégio da Purificação, Évora, from 1617 to 1618. The name is variously given as Querano, Cheran, Kenas.[262]

CHARLES KELLAGHAN had been in the college for two years in 1615.[263]

BERNARD KELLY returned to Ireland some time between 1590 and 1615.[264]

EDMOND KELLY SJ, from diocese of Clonfert, received minor orders on 25 July 1632, entered the Jesuits the same years, attended the Irish college, went to University of Évora for a course in Philosophy and Theology. He returned to St Patrick's College, was sent to the Azores to teach moral theology. He was back again in the Irish College in 1639 and was rector, 1655–8.[265]

PATRICK KELLY, student of St Patrick's College, Lisbon, was bishop of Richmond, Virginia from 1820 until his appointment to the see of Waterford in 1822. He died two years later.[266]

---

254 LIS/2, 4. **255** Fenning, 2, p. 69. **256** LIS/4. **257** LIS/7. **258** Anthony Cogan, *The diocese of Meath, ancient and modern*, iii (Dublin, 1870), pp 243–5. **259** Fenning, 2, p. 69. **260** Ibid; LIS/7. **261** Fenning, 3, p. 149. **262** Fenning, 1, p. 112; LIS/7. **263** LIS/4. **264** Ibid. **265** LIS/7; G. da C., p. 427. **266** O'Boyle, op. cit., p. 180.

DANIEL KEOHANE, ordained on 9 March 1698, said Foundation Masses from 1698 to 1699.[267]

CHARLES KIRWAN received the *viaticum* of 4 *milreis* to return to Ireland on 24 March 1625.[268]

RICHARD KIRWAN was ordained on 8 June 1755.[269]

JOHN LAMPORT received minor orders on 23 August 1618.[270]

RICHARD LAMPORT was ordained on 2 April 1650.[271]

THOMAS LAMPORT was made sub-deacon on 20 September 1642.[272]

DAVID LANGAN, son of Cornelius Langan and Elisia Inani (*sic*), of town of Ardpatrick, County Limerick, was ordained on 23 December 1619.[273]

HUGH LACY died some time between 1590 and 1615.[274]

LOURENCO LEA SJ was born on 10 August 1584, in Waterford, son of John Lea and Elizabeth Walsh. He studied in the Irish college before he entered the Jesuits in 1604. He went on to Salamanca in 1603. After some years in Germany and the Low Countries he returned to Ireland and became vicar-general of Waterford.[275]

DOMINICK LENEO, son of Edward Leneo and Ilena Afonse, was ordained on 23 September 1600. He was from Cahre (*sic*).[276]

WILLIAM LENEO, son of Marques Leneo and Margaret Escasey, was given the tonsure on 23 September 1600.[277]

REV. MR LENNON studied at the college as an extern up to 1807.[278]

DANIEL LEONARD, son of William Leonard and Helena Joana, ordained on 21 July 1615, was from diocese of Limerick.[279]

MICHAEL LEYDEN ordained on 22 March 1699, celebrated Foundation masses in the college from 1699 to 1702.[280]

BARTHOLOMEW LINEGAR was ordained on 7 January 1725.[281]

---

267 Fenning, 2, p. 69; LIS/2, 4. **268** G. da C., p. 412. **269** Fenning, 3, p. 149. **270** LIS/7. **271** Fenning, 1, p. 112. **272** Ibid. **273** Ibid.LIS/4, 7. **274** LIS/4. **275** G. da C., p. 428; Finegan, 'Biographical Dictionary', pp 86–7; MT 1615. **276** Fenning, 1, p. 112. **277** Ibid. **278** DDA File 117/7, letter from Joseph Joy Deane to Dr Troy dated 14 Mar. 1807. **279** Fenning, 1, p. 113; G. da C., p. 410; LIS/2, 7. **280** Fenning, 2, p. 69; LIS/2, 4. **281** Fenning, 2.

THE STUDENTS

JOHN LINEGAR, ordained on 31 December 1694, became archbishop of Dublin (1734–57).[282]

FRANCIS LINNAN was ordained on 20 October 1833.[283]

MICHAEL LINNAN received minor orders on 21 September 1833.[284]

LINSE – See LYNCH.

MALACHY LOGHLIN, ordained before 1624, was a secular priest in Ireland, 1625.[285]

ANDREW LONDON became sub-deacon on 18 September 1649.[286]

ROBERT LONG, son of Bartholomew Longe and Alonsa Moore, had been three years in the college in 1615 and was 28 years old.[287]

CHARLES LUHER OFM left the seminary some time between 1590 and 1615.[288]

ANTHONY LYNCH OP, son of Nicholas and Juliana Martin, diocese of Tuam, became a sub-deacon on 18 December 1599. He was a merchant for two or three years, studied Arts in St Patrick's and went on to Salamanca in 1602.[289]

DOMINICK LYNCH, ordained on 19 March 1698, left for Ireland on 7 July 1699.[290]

EDMUND LYNCH was ordained on 9 November 1645.[291]

JAMES LYNCH (I) was ordained on 19 September 1655.[292]

JAMES LYNCH (II), son of Richard Lence and Joana Danochui (Donahoe), was ordained on 4 January 1618; from the diocese of Limerick.[293]

JOHN LYNCH (I) was ordained on 30 May 1711.[294]

JOHN LYNCH (II) celebrated masses in St Patrick's from 1675–82 and had faculties to hear confessions, 1681–2.[295]

---

282 Fenning, *Register, 1704*. **283** Fenning, 3, p. 149. **284** Fenning, 3. **285** LIS/4. **286** Fenning, 1, 113. **287** LIS/4. **288** G. da C., op. cit., p. 407. **289** Fenning, 1, p. 113; O'Doherty, *Arch. Hib.* 2 (1913) 13–14; G da C., p. 408. **290** Fenning, 2, p. 70; LIS/2, 4. **291** Fenning, 1, p. 113. **292** Ibid. **293** Ibid; LIS/2, 4. **294** Fenning, 2, p. 70. **295** LIS/4.

NICHOLAS LYNCH OP, of Galway, was a student at St Patrick's before 1615 and in 1625 a preacher in Ireland. He was Prior provincial (1627–32) and died at St Malo, 1639.[296]

THOMAS LYNCH (I) (also called FitzAnthony) was ordained on 16 July 1679. He said Foundation masses in the college from 1676 to 1681. He lived in the city of Galway in 1704, aged 49, at New Tower, parish of St Nicholas.[297]

THOMAS LYNCH (II), son of Stephen Lynch and Catherine, entered the college in 1703 and joined the Jesuits. He was ordained on 10 February 1709, and left for Brazil the same year.[298]

WALTER LYNCH, ordained some time before 1625, became bishop of Clonfert (1647–63). He went into exile in 1648 and died in Hungary. He is associated with the devotion there to Our Lady of Gyor.[299]

VASCO LYNCH, a secular priest, theologian and preacher in Ireland around 1625.[300]

JOHN LYNHAM was ordained on 28 December 1618; he was the son of Anthony and Isabel.[301]

DENIS LYNE celebrated Foundation masses, 1705–6, when he was aged 28 years.[302]

JOHN MAC CABE was ordained on 12 August 1736.[303]

JAMES MAC CARTHY returned home in 1776 from his studies in Lisbon.[303a]

HUGH MC CLOSKEY, listed as a subscriber to *The lives of the saints* by Alban Butler, 3rd ed. (Dublin 1802) and his address is given as St Patrick's, Lisbon. He was later curate in Strabane.[304]

EDMUND MAC CORMACK, ordained on 11 January 1705, is recorded as saying Foundation masses, 1705–7.[305]

EDMUND MAC ROGHAN was ordained on 23 October 1735.[306]

296 Ibid; See H. Fenning, *Coll. Hib.*, 42 (2000), p. 54.   **297** Fenning, 2, p. 70; *Register*, 1704; LIS/4.   **298** Fenning, 2; LIS/3, 4; G. da C., p. 365.   **299** LIS/4; Brady, *Episcopal succession*, ii (Rome, 1876), pp 216–17.   **300** LIS/4.   **301** Fenning, 1, p. 113.   **302** LIS/4.   **303** Fenning, 2, p. 70.   **303a** *Reportorium Novum*, 1/2 (1956), p. 489.   **304** This information supplied by Father Hugh Fenning.   **305** Ibid.,; LIS/4.   **306** Fenning, 2, p. 70.

THE STUDENTS

CHARLES MAC DONNELL was ordained on 13 June 1732.[307]

JOHN MC EVILLY was ordained on 3 July 1831.[308]

ROCHUS MAC GEOGHEGAN OP (Rochus [Roque] da Cruz, Ross and Roch also found) was born at Moycashel, County Westmeath, in 1577. He left Ireland for Lisbon 1590, aged 13 years on the recommendation of the rector at Lisbon. He studied 'litterae humaniores' for five months in St Patrick's early in 1600, and went on to Salamanca in June 1601. He was bishop of Kildare, 1629–44.[309]

DENIS MAC KELGHAN returned to Ireland some time between 1590 and 1615.[310]

GEORGE MAC KENNA was ordained on 30 May 1733.[311]

MACMAHON, MAHON – See MAC MAHON, and MATHEWS.

PATRICK MAC MAHON, ordained 1692, lived Clontarf, Dublin, aged 36, in 1704.[311a]

PATRICK MAC MAHON was in Lisbon when the earthquake struck. He resigned as professor due to ill health; was related to Archbishop Ross MacMahon, of Armagh; died at Red Cow, Dundalk, 1765, and was buried in Castletown graveyard there.[312]

MACMULLAN – See MULLEN.

EDMUND MADDEN, ordained on 19 May 1674; son of Thomas and Una Madum, a native of County Galway and the diocese of Clonfert.[313]

ANDREW MAGAGHRAN, ordained in 1651 in Lisbon, in 1704 was listed as living in Diraney, parish of Dromlane, County Cavan.[314]

BERNARD MAGEE came from the diocese of Down and Connor; a former student of St Patrick's College and ordained in 1753. He wrote a letter to the rector of St Patrick's from Seville in 1808.[315]

DENIS MAGRATH was a collegian in 1624.[316]

---

307 Fenning, 2, p. 71.   **308** Fenning, 3, p. 150.   **309** G. da C., p. 408; T.S. Flynn OP, *The Irish Dominicans, 1536–1641* (Dublin, 1993), p. 108.   **310** LIS/4.   **311** Fenning, 2, p. 71.   **311a** *Register, 1704.*   **312** Details received from Father Hugh Fenning.   **313** Fenning, 2, p. 71.   **314** *Register, 1704.*   **315** Details from Father Hugh Fenning again.   **316** LIS/4.

DERMOT MC GRATH OSA was a student in the Irish College, Lisbon, and later provincial of the Augustinians in Ireland *c.*1625.[317]

MATTHEW MAGRATH, son of Haden Machra and Unina Macarring from the diocese of Killaloe, was given Minor Orders on 21 September 1596 and belonged to the household of Bishop Cornelius O Mulryan.[318]

MICHAEL MAGRATH was a collegian in St Patrick's in 1624 when he signed a letter, with others, to the General of the Jesuits in Rome.[319]

THOMAS MAGRATH OFM was ordained on 4 February 1616; he was in Ireland in 1625.[320]

WILLIAM MAGRATH SJ (Guilhermo da Cruz, Cragh or Crevaeous) was born 1580. He was from Burges, near Cahir, County Tipperary, archdiocese of Cashel. A collegian of St Patrick's, he entered the Jesuits in Coimbra in 1605, studied there for four years and was ordained in 1616. He became rector of the Irish college (1622–4) and returned to Ireland in 1625. He died in Limerick on 1 November 1651.[321]

RAYMOND MAGUIRE was ordained on 18 March 1753.[322]

MAHON – See MACMAHON and MATHEWS.

JOHN MALLON, received Minor Orders on 1 February 1795; son of John and Anne Durns, native of the parish of Ballinderry, archdiocese of Armagh.[323]

THOMAS MALLEY, son of Patrick Mayleus and Maria Cafoios, was born in New Ross, diocese of Ferns; he went to college in Évora on 27 July 1598, when 20 years old.[324]

MALACHY MANAGHAN was ordained on 21 September 1835.[325]

NICHOLAS MANDEVILLE, son of Dominick Mandeville and Isabel Tobin, town of Ballydine, diocese of Lismore, was ordained on 6 September 1621.[326]

WILLIAM MANNING was ordained on 21 October 1833.[327]

---

317 Ibid. **318** Fenning, 1, p. 113. **319** LIS/4; see Dermot BRYN (Brown) above. **320** G. da C., p. 407; LIS/4. **321** G. da C., pp 423–4; Finegan, 'Biographical Dictionary', p. 108. **322** Fenning, 3, p. 151. **323** Ibid. **324** LIS/4. **325** Fenning, 3, p. 151. **326** Fenning, 1, p. 113. **327** Fenning, 3, p. 151.

THE STUDENTS

JOHN MANNING – See MORRISON; also Chapter 7.

RICHARD MARKEY was ordained deacon on 22 December 1646.[328]

MATER DEI – See Carlo della Mater Dei.

ANDREW MATHEWS, ordained on 23 September 1686, was son of Thomas Matheod and Alison Halpenny of the parish of Navan, diocese of Meath; said Masses in the college up to 12 June 1691, when he returned to Ireland; appointed parish priest of Oristown in 1704.[329]

PATRICK MATHEWS, ordained on 13 October 1697, began to celebrate Foundation masses the following month.[330]

ROGER MATHEWS was ordained on 8 June 1688.[331]

THOMAS MATHEWS, who entered the Jesuits in 1600, had possibly been a student at the college before that.[332]

JAMES MEAGH (MIAGH), son of Dominick Miach and Elizabeth Lange of Cork, studied at Lisbon in 1598 and at Salamanca from 1601. He returned to Ireland before 1615.[333]

JAMES MEEHAN SJ was ordained on 13 September 1801.[334]

JAMES MOHERY, from the diocese of Kilmore, went to Lisbon in 1650 and was ordained on 4 March 1651.[335]

LAURENCE MOLLOY was ordained on 18 June 1713.[336]

THOMAS MONSIN, a secular priest, returned to Ireland some time between 1590 and 1615.[337]

JOHN MOORE SJ (I) studied Humanities in the college prior to entering the Jesuits in 1600. Born in Duleek, County Meath, in 1582, he studied at the University of Coimbra and was recalled to Ireland and appointed to the Connacht residency until 1625. He then transferred to Dublin and Drogheda, before returning eventually to Galway. He died in 1652.[338]

JOHN MOORE (II) was ordained on 10 August 1717.[339]

328 Fenning, 1, p. 113.   **329** Fenning, 2, p. 72; name also found as Mahon; *Register, 1704*; *Meath List*, p. 1242; MT 13 Jan. 1685; LIS/2, 4.   **330** Fenning, 2; also found as Mahon or MacMahon; LIS/2.4.   **331** Fenning, 2.   **332** MT 1615.   **333** O'Doherty, *Arch. Hib.* 2 (1913) 8–9; LIS/4.   **334** Fenning, 3, p. 152.   **335** Ibid., 1, pp 106 and 113–4.   **336** Ibid, (2), p. 72.   **337** LIS/4.   **338** Ibid.; F. Finegan, 'Biographical Dictionary', p. 114; MT, Precis 1621.   **339** Fenning, 2, p. 72.

JOHN MORAN was ordained on 3 July 1831.[340]

CHRISTOPHER MORGAN was ordained on 24 October 1706.[341]

WALTER MOROGH, a collegian c.1624.[342]

MICHAEL MORRIS SJ was a student of the college and entered Jesuits in 1607 when he was 17 years old. He studied at Coimbra and after ordination in 1615 or 1616 he acted as minister in the Irish College, Seville. He returned to Ireland. Apparently dismissed from the Order in 1630, he set out for Rome that year to put his complaints against the Order and all regular clergy in Ireland. He is identified with Michael Cantwell who disappears from the Jesuit catalogue and was also known as Morais.[343]

JOHN MORRISON: this student's name is Mannion but appears as Morrison in DDA. He was in the college in 1822 and joined the household of Viscount Manique that same year and was resident in his palace and was from the diocese of Elphin. He was one of the three concerned priests who wrote to Dr. Troy about the bad state of the college. The others were Thomas Nevil and Patrick O'Connor Hay.[344]

JOHN MOURA (MORE) SJ, born in 1582, was from the diocese of Meath and was a student at the college in Lisbon. He entered the Jesuits on 25 April 1600, attended the University of Coimbra for the Philosophy course, returned to St Patrick's, where he spent three years, and was recorded as '*companheiro*' to the rector, Cornelio da Rocha.[345]

NICHOLAS MOYDELL, ordained in 1619, was in the college until 1624.[346]

BARNABY MULLEN was ordained on 18 July 1802. Probably the Mr Mullen, who delivered a letter in 1797 from the archbishop of Dublin to the college in which it was stated he wished to become a 'subject' of St Patrick's.[347]

DAVID MULLEN became sub-deacon on 18 September 1649.[348]

---

340 Ibid., 3, p. 152. **341** Ibid., 2, p. 72. **342** LIS/4. **343** G. da. C., p. 430; Finegan, op. cit., pp 23–24. **344** DDA letter to Troy 1822. The name is mistakenly given as Morrison but should be John Mannion, from the diocese of Elphin, 1822, Details of John Mannion will be found in Chapter 7. **345** G. da. C., p. 430. **346** Ibid. p. 262. **347** Fenning, 3, p. 152; DDA letter, 12 June 1797 from Troy to Daly. **348** Fenning, 1, p. 114.

THE STUDENTS

JAMES MULLEN was recommended to the rector of St Patrick's by Father Knoles, superior of the Jesuits in Ireland, on 27 February 1725.[349]

EDMUND MURPHY was ordained on 22 September 1804.[350]

EDMUND (EDWARD) MURPHY was nephew of Archbishop Patrick Russell of Dublin. He arrived at the seminary before 14 May 1698, recommended by the General in Rome, Thyrsus Gonzalez. It was said that he was 'brainy'.[351]

JOHN MURPHY was ordained on 10 May 1795, and later became Bishop of Cork (1815–47).[352]

MARTIN MURPHY became sub-deacon on 18 December 1694, returned to Ireland in 1695.[353]

MICHAEL MURPHY, son of Michael and Mary Furlong, was baptised in the parish of Duncormack, County Wexford, diocese of Ferns. He was ordained on 21 July 1799.[354]

PETER MURPHY was in the list of seculars, returned to Ireland between 1590 and 1615.[355]

RICHARD MURPHY was ordained on 12 June 1695, said Foundation masses from then until 31 March 1697, when he returned to Ireland. In 1704 he was living in Cook Street, Dublin, aged 38.[356]

THOMAS MURPHY, ordained on 17 February 1680, said masses in the college until 1683.[357]

WILLIAM NAGLE, ordained on 18 May 1589, returned to Ireland some time after that date; a cousin of Nicholas Dubin, also a collegian in St Patrick's.[358]

PETER NASH SJ, son of William Nosse and Ilena Molroney, was ordained on 8 June 1607. He was born Fethard, archdiocese of Cashel, in 1561. He entered the Jesuits and was known as Pedro Inácio, attended the Irish College as a boy, and was rector, minister, teacher and proctor for long periods in the college during his career.[359]

---

349 LIS/4.   **350** Fenning, 3, p. 152.   **351** MT 4 May 1689; LIS/2, 4.
352 Fenning, 3, p. 152. See Chapter 7.   **353** Fenning, 2, p. 72; LIS/4.
354 Fenning, 3, pp 152–3.   **355** LIS/4.   **356** Fenning, 2, p. 72; *Register, 1704*; LIS/2.   **357** Fenning; LIS/2, 4.   **358** Fenning, 1, p. 114; G. da C. pp 209, 409.
359 Fenning 1; G. da C., p. 99; Finegan, 'Biographical Dictionary', p. 119.

THOMAS NASH, son of Robert Nash and Stacia Forte, of Wexford, received the tonsure on 23 September 1600.[360]

DENIS NIELLAN was made sub-deacon on 20 December 1587. From the diocese of Killaloe.[361]

JOHN NELLY was ordained on 8 July 1657.[362]

RUPERT NETTERVILLE, born on 5 April 1626, studied at the college and was later spiritual director there.[363]

JOHN NEVIL, ordained on 6 September 1676, celebrated Foundation masses in the college until 1679.[364]

ROBERT NEVIL SJ, born on 5 April 1626, and ordained in 1655. Entered the Society of Jesus the same year, studied at University of Évora and was minister and proctor in St Patrick's until 1662, when he left for Madeira, where he died in 1677.[365]

THOMAS NEVIL, from diocese of Ferns, was in the college in 1822; he was one of the signatories of letter to Dr Troy regarding the state of the college.[366]

JAMES NITELL OFM became a Franciscan and left the college some time between 1590 and 1615.[367]

GERALD NOGLY was ordained on 19 March 1641.[368]

ANDREW NOLAN SJ, born in County Galway 1582, studied at the college before entering the Jesuits in 1600. Died in 1652.[369]

GASPAR NOLAN returned to Ireland from the college some time between 1590 and 1615.[370]

GILBERT NUGENT took minor orders on 3 June 1616.[371]

OLIVER NUGENT, from Meath diocese, ordained 19 March 1641, was appointed parish priest of Beauparc in 1690.[372]

DANIEL O' BRENNAN was among those collegians who died between 1590 and 1615.[373]

---

360 Fenning, 1. **361** Ibid. **362** Ibid. **363** LIS/4; Finegan, op. cit., p. 122. **364** LIS/4; Fenning, 2, p. 73. **365** Fenning, 1, p. 114; G. da C. p. 325; Finegan, op. cit., p. 122. **366** DDA, letter to Troy, 1822, see Chapter 7 LIS/6. **367** LIS/4. **368** LIS/7. **369** LIS/4. **370** LIS/4. **371** LIS/7. **372** Ibid.; *Meath List*, p. 1246. **373** LIS/4.

THE STUDENTS

ANDREW O'BRIEN took minor orders on 29 June 1679 and final ordination 26 December 1685. He attended the Royal College of the Purification at the University of Évora. At first glance it appeared there were two students named Andrew O'Brien. In spite of the long time between minor orders and final ordination, I think there was just the one.[374]

CORNELIUS O'BRIEN was ordained on 5 December 1728.[375]

MAURICE O'BRIEN, from diocese of Killaloe, was ordained on 3 August 1806.[376]

RICHARD O'BRIEN took minor orders on 29 June 1679.[377]

O'CARROLL – See CARNE, DANIEL.

CLEMENT O'CONNOR was ordained on 21 April 1844.[378]

PATRICK O'CONNOR HAY, from Dublin diocese, had been a collegian in St Patrick's. He was preceptor of the dukes of Cadaval and Lafoës in 1822, and resided in the house of the former. He was one of the signatories of the 1822 letter sent to Dr Troy regarding the bad state of the college.[379]

JOHN O'CURRIN, son of Maurice and Leonora Archer, was ordained on 27 March 1742, attended the College of the Purification in the University of Évora, and was the *amanuensis* of the Rev. Miguel de Almeida and Rev. Diego Pacheco in the preparation of the *Tractatus Theologicus Moralis de Sacramento Poenitentiae*, c.1741.[380]

O'DALY – See DALY.

CONSTANTINE O'DONNELL, son of Terence Odonolio and Sylvia Duilha (also found as Nigul), native of town das Monias, diocese of Lismore, was ordained on 23 December 1619 and was in Ireland in 1625.[381]

LUKE O'DONNELL was ordained on 9 October 1740.[382]

DENIS O'DRISCOLL, son of Dermot and Honora MacCarthy, was ordained on 9 September 1781.[383]

---

[374] Fenning, 2, p. 73. [375] Ibid. [376] Fenning, 3, p. 153. [377] Ibid., 2, p. 73. [378] Ibid., 3, p. 153. [379] DDA, letter from three concerned priests, dated 1822, to Dr Troy. [380] Fenning, 3, p. 153; G. da C., p. 54, there is a conflict of dates here as G. da C. gives 1714, which may be a misprint for 1741. He also asserts that O'Currin was from diocese of Ferns. [381] Ibid., 1, p. 115; LIS/4. [382] Fenning, 3, p. 153. [383] Ibid.

SIMON OF THE HOLY SPIRIT O'HALLAGHAN OP was a student in St Patrick's from 1584 to 1591 when he became a Dominican. He re-established the Order in Munster.[383a]

WILLIAM O'HANLY was given the tonsure on 17 September 1784.[384]

THOMAS O'HURGAN returned to Ireland between 1590 and 1615.[385]

JOSEPH O'KEEFE was ordained on 18 July 1802.[386]

PATRICK O'KELLY, from Dublin, ordained on 18 July 1802, left the college in consequence of indisposition, was captured on the way home, returned to Lisbon and left a second time in 1804.[387]

WILLIAM O'KELLY, son of James O'Kelly and Maria Thomasia Josefa, was ordained on 20 June 1773. A native of the town of Moura and diocese of Beja, Portugal, he was parish priest of Amareleja, near Évora, 1772–89.[388]

MAGNUS OLTACH, a secular priest, returned home to Ireland some time between 1590 and 1616.[389]

EDWARD O'MEALY was ordained on 20 October 1833.[390]

JOHN O'MEARA was ordained on 18 July 1802.[391]

JAMES O'SHAUGHNESSY, from diocese of Killaloe, was ordained on 13 January 1805.[392]

DANIEL O'SULLIVAN, ordained on 23 March 1624, was the son of Daniel O'Sullivan and Joana Mahona (also Conel).[393]

ANDREW PEPPARD received the tonsure and minor orders on 18 September 1676.[394]

GEORGE PEPPARD was ordained on 10 March 1697.[395]

ROBERT PLUNKETT was in third-year Philosophy on 5 June 1615.[396]

383a T.S. Flynn, op. cit, *The Irish Dominicans, 1536–1641*, pp 100, 130. Flynn lists fifteen other students of the college who became Dominicans between 1593 and 1615 – John White, Anthony Lynch, William Talbot, John White, Ross MacGeoghegan, Thomas Bathe, Michael Brown, William Harold, Nicholas Lynch, Stephen Lynch, Barnabas Murphy, Peter Martin, Thaddeus Murphy, Thomas Brandon and James Nelan. **384** Fenning, 3, p. 154. **385** LIS/4. **386** Fenning, 3, p. 154. **387** Ibid; D.D.A. **388** Ibid; G. da C., p. 24. **389** LIS/4. **390** Fenning, 3, p. 154. **391** Ibid. **392** Fenning, 3, p.155. **393** Fenning, 1, p. 115. **394** Fenning, 2, p. 73. **395** Ibid. **396** LIS/4.

THE STUDENTS

ANDREW PORTO was ordained on 19 September 1655.[397]

PETER POTRO was given minor orders on 4 April 1616.[398]

JAMES POWER was ordained on 30 September 1644.[399]

WILLIAM POWER received minor orders on 18 December 1648.[400]

JAMES PRENDERGAST was given minor orders on 19 September 1664.[401]

WILLIAM PRENDERGAST was ordained on 6 January 1618.[402]

CYPRIAN PURCELL OSA, was a student in St Patrick's and later, in 1625, an Augustinian friar and preacher in Ireland.[403]

DENIS PURCELL, son of Thomas and Elena, became a Deacon on 24 May 1603 and left for Ireland some time before 1615.[404]

THOMAS PURCELL, son of Denis and Bella Comerford, Waterford, received the tonsure on 23 September 1600.[405]

QUEITROT — See DA CRUZ.

QUELLIO(S) — See KELLY.

QUINAO — See KEENAN.

DANIEL QUINN celebrated Foundation masses in the college, 1697–8.[406]

WILLIAM QUINN (I) (also found as Guinn), ordained on 9 June 1827, had been a student of the English College of Sts. Peter and Paul, in Lisbon.[407]

WILLIAM QUINN (II) was ordained on 21 September 1830.[408]

JOHN QUISANO was a student in St Patrick's before 1615, when he joined the Jesuits.[409]

RAYMOND, son of Raymond and Anastasia of Derry City, was ordained on 4 February 1608.[410]

MR REDMOND may have been from Dublin. He is mentioned in a letter from the rector to Dr Troy, in May 1803, as being resolved to leave the college shortly; he was a member of the staff.[411]

---

97 Fenning, 1, p. 115. **398** LIS/7. **399** Fenning, 1, p. 115. **400** Ibid. **401** Fenning, 2, p. 73. **402** Fenning, 1, p. 115. **403** LIS/4. **404** Fenning, 1, p. 115; LIS/4. **405** Fenning, 1. **406** LIS/4. **407** Fenning, 3, p. 148. **408** Ibid., 3, p. 155. **409** G. da C., p. 431. **410** Fenning, 1, p. 115. **411** DDA, letter Crotty to Troy, dated 7 May 1803.

AIDAN REDMOND, ordained on 26 April 1673, was living in Clonleigh, parish of Old Ross, County Wexford in 1704, aged 55 years. He said Foundation masses in the college from 1673 to 1679.[412]

EDWARD REDMOND, ordained in Lisbon by Bishop Sleyne in his oratory on 3 March 1708, was a student in the college from 1705.[413]

LUKE REDMOND was ordained on 27 September 1655.[414]

MAURICE REGAN, son of Donnell Regan and Onora Carch, ordained on 8 June 1607, was a student, also, at the College of the Purification in Évora.[415]

GERARD (also Gerald) REILLY was ordained on 22 March 1699 and was possibly the parish priest of Killucan in 1704 who died in 1760.[416]

JAMES REILLY was ordained on 21 March 1700; possibly parish priest of Lobinstown, County Meath, appointed 1704.[417]

MAURICE REILLY received minor orders on 14 September 1660.[418]

RICHARDUS SANCTI VICTORIS OSA was a student of the Irish College, Lisbon, before 1625.[419]

WILLIAM RIORDAN, ordained on 6 March 1622. The name is also found as Cridan.[420]

VALENTINE RIVERS was ordained on 19 March 1696. He was listed in 1704 as living in James's Street, aged 32 years, parish of St Catherine. He was in dispute for some years with the archbishop of Dublin, Edmund Byrne, regarding his claim to be the parish priest of St Catherine's.[421]

CORNELIO DA ROCHA was a student at St Patrick's and rector from 1609 to 1619.[422]

JOHN ROCHE SJ, from diocese of Ferns, was ordained on 4 January 1618.[423]

NICHOLAS ROCHE (1) received minor orders in December 1666.[424]

---

412 Fenning, 2, p. 73; LIS/4; *Register, 1704*. 413 LIS/4, 6; G. da. C., p. 363; Fenning, 2, pp 73–4. 414 Fenning, 1, p. 116. 415 Ibid; LIS/4. 416 Fenning, 2 p.74; *Meath List*, p. 1249. 417 Fenning, 2; *Meath List*, ibid; LIS/2, 4; G. da C., p. 332. 418 LIS/7. 419 LIS/4. 420 LIS/7; G. da C., p. 411. 421 Fenning, 2, p. 74; *Register, 1704*; see also H. Fenning, in Kelly and Keogh (eds), *History of the Catholic diocese of Dublin*, p. 181, on the dispute with the archbishop. 422 See Chapter 3. 423 Fenning, 1, p. 116; LIS/8. 424 Fenning, 2, p. 74; LIS/7; MT 1666.

NICHOLAS ROCHE (II), from diocese of Ferns, ordained on 29 September 1685; he lived in Ballynegora, County Wexford, aged 45, in 1704.[425]

RICHARD ROCHE, ordained on 11 May 1623, was son of John da Rich and Joanna Sex. He signed the memorial in 1624.[426]

THEOBALD ROCHE, from Limerick, ordained on 11 November 1629, was a son of David Roche and Margaret Hifernan, from parish of Kilfinan, diocese of Limerick.[427]

JOHN ROIS was ordained on 6 January 1618; may be the same as John Roche above.[428]

PATRICK ROQUE died some time between 1590 and 1615.[429]

MICHAEL ROSSITER, from Wexford, diocese of Ferns, was ordained on 27 December 1671. In the 1704 list he is aged 56 and lived at Rongheen, parish of Killinick. He became bishop of Ferns (1698–1709).[430]

PATRICK RUSSELL, ordained on 12 June 1654, later archbishop of Dublin (1683–92), was uncle of one of the students, Edward Murphy.[431]

JAMES RYAN was ordained 1623.[432]

WILLIAM RYAN was ordained on 9 October 1740.[33]

GEORGE ST. LAWRENCE, born 1675, celebrated Foundation masses, 1702–6.[434]

LAWRENCE ST LAWRENCE was ordained on 17 April 1628.[435]

JOHN SCAEL said Foundation masses from 1676 to 1682.[436]

BARTHOLOMEW SCALY, who lived in Dunshaughlin, aged 48, was ordained in 1684 in Coimbra.[437]

HUBERT SHANLY, ordained on 21 September 1765, son of Daniel Shanly and Elizabeth O'Ferrall, native of Annaghduff, diocese of Ardagh, attended the English College of Sts Peter and Paul after 1764.[438]

EDWARD SHEE was ordained on 25 March 1730.[439]

---

425 Ibid; *Register, 1704*.   **426** Fenning, 1, p. 116; G. da C., p. 262; LIS/4,7.   **427** LIS/4, 7; G. da. C., p. 262.   **428** LIS/7.   **429** LIS/4.   **430** Fenning, 2, p. 74; *Register, 1704*.   **431** Fenning, 1, p. 116.   **432** LIS/7.   **433** Fenning, 3, p.156.   **434** LIS/4,7; G. da C., p. 363.   **435** LIS/7.   **436** LIS/4, 7.   **437** *Register, 1704*.   **438** Fenning, 3, p. 156.   **439** Fenning, 2, p. 74.

MARK SHEE (name also given as Marcos Se), ordained on 15 November 1682, celebrated Foundation masses in the college 1686 to 1688, and returned to Ireland on 8 July 1688. In 1704, aged 45, he was living in Derrynehensy, parish of Sheepstown, Killkirill, Aghvillar, Kilkredey, County Kilkenny.[440]

PATRICK SHEE (I) was ordained on 8 June 1685 and celebrated Foundation masses, 1688–91.[441]

PATRICK SHEE (II), ordained in 1690, was born in Kilkenny City and lived there in 1704. He was then 44 years of age and attached to St Patrick's there.[442]

WILLIAM SHEEHAN, from the diocese of Cloyne, was ordained in Lisbon in 1668. In 1704, age 62 years, he lived in Garret-mac-Garret, parish of Killboin, Castlemagner and Ballyclough.[443]

BARTHOLOMEW SHERLOCK, ordained on 1 April 1753, was from the diocese of Dublin, and was later parish priest of St Catherine's, Meath Street, and dean of Dublin, he died on 3 July 1806.[444]

WILLIAM SHERRY was ordained on 17 March 1816.[445]

DENIS SHINE, son of Maurice Shein and Anna Lyons from Clonmel, diocese of Lismore, went on to Salamanca and took the 'oath' there in 1607, aged 27 years. He left for Ireland before 1615.[446]

MICHAEL SHINNORS was ordained on 18 July 1802.[447]

DOMINICK DA SILVA (CARTHY), ordained on 23 September 1623, was a son of Maria da Silva and Maurice Carte (Carthy), native of Ireland.[448]

THOMAS SIMON, son of John, received minor orders on 19 December 1587 from Bishop Cornelius O'Mulryan in the cathedral, Lisbon.[449]

THOMAS SIMORO presented for minor orders in December 1666.[450]

JOHN SINNOTT, OFM (John FitzPhilip) was a student of the Irish College and was a preacher in Ireland in 1625.[451]

---

440 Fenning, 2, p. 75; LIS/2, 4; *Register*, 1704. **441** Fenning, 2; LIS/4. **442** LIS/4; *Register*, 1704. **443** *Register*, 1704. **444** Fenning, 3, p. 156; LIS/2; *Reportorium Novum*, i, 2(1956), p. 409. **445** Fenning, 3, pp 156. **446** LIS/4. **447** Fenning, 3, pp 156–7. **448** Fenning, 3, p. 116. **449** Ibid. **450** MT 1666. **451** G. da C., p. 407; LIS/4.

RICHARD SINNOT OFM, a student of the Irish College, was a close friend of Father Luke Wadding, OFM.[452]

JAMES SKERRIT, ordained in August 1621; spent five years in the seminary of St Patrick and also attended the University of Évora.[453]

GREGORY SKERRITT was given permission to hear confessions in 1633, as his Portuguese was considered sufficient.[454]

JOHN SMITH (FERREIRA) was ordained on 29 September 1685. In 1704 he was living in Dunsany, aged 50, parish of Dunsany, Kilmessan, Scurlockstown, Tribly, Balsoone and Assey, diocese of Meath.[455]

MICHAEL SMITH (FERREIRA) said Foundation masses in 1684 in the college; he went on to Évora and received his doctorate there.[456]

ALEXIS STAFFORD, ordained on 10 August 1675, was in the college until 1679. He was dean of Christ Church, Dublin, where he said mass from 1689–90.[457]

JOHN STAFFORD, from the diocese of Ferns.[458]

NICHOLAS STAFFORD, ordained on 12 May 1680, celebrated the Foundation masses, 1681–5.[459]

THEOBALD STAPLETON was ordained before 1612. He was the founder of the Irish Colleges at Madrid and Seville. He spent a short time in the Irish College, Lisbon. He was martyred at Cashel cathedral in 1647, cut down while he distributed Holy Communion to the congregation.[460]

WILLIAM STONE was ordained on 29 September 1716.[461]

ANDREW STUDI died some time between 1590 and 1615.[462]

NICHOLAS SWEETMAN, ordained on 18 September 1717, became bishop of Ferns, 1745–86.[463]

THOMAS SYMONS was ordained on 4 July 1671.[464]

---

452 LIS/4. **453** LIS/4. **454** LIS/7. **455** Fenning, 2, p. 66 as John Ferreira; *Register, 1704*, p. 202. **456** LIS/2, 4; MT 25 Mar. 1684. **457** Fenning, 2, p. 75; LIS/2, 4. **458** LIS/4., no date given. **459** Fenning, 2, p. 75. **460** D. Murphy, *Our martyrs* (Dublin, 1868), p. 307; G. da C., p. 89; T.F. Walsh, op. cit., p. 58. **461** Fenning, 2, p. 75. **462** LIS/4. **463** Fenning, 2, p. 75; LIS/4. **464** Fenning, 2, p. 75.

PETER TAAFFE had been two years in the seminary and studied three courses in 1615.[465]

DIDACUS (JAMES) TALBOT, a secular priest and vicar-general in the diocese of Kildare, was ordained before 1625 and had been a student of the college.[466]

GEORGE TALBOT, from the diocese of Meath, was ordained 23 September 1633, and was a student in the college from 1624 to 1633.[467]

JAMES TALBOT, son of John and Leonora Gariona, from the diocese of Meath, was ordained on 19 July 1615.[468]

JOHN TALBOT SJ, born 1610, was in the college before 1625, when he joined the Jesuits; he studied at the University of Coimbra, returned to Ireland and lived at his mother's house in Carton, County Kildare.[469]

MATHEW TALBOT SJ was in the college in 1624. He became a Jesuit.[470]

PETER TALBOT SJ he was in the college before 1635, when he entered the Jesuits; ordained in April 1648 and studied at the University of Coimbra. Described in a contemporary report, from Lisbon, to Rome as talented, prudent and possessing sound judgment. He later became archbishop of Dublin (1669–80). He espoused the cause of Charles II, much to the disapproval of the General of the Order in Rome. He subsequently left the Order. Born in 1618, he was from Carton, near Maynooth, and was a younger brother of John Talbot, above. He died in prison in Dublin Castle, on 15 November 1680.[471]

PATRICK TALLON received minor orders on 19 September 1664.[472]

ROBERT TAYLOR (I) was ordained on 20 May 1618; the son of George Tailero and Alisone Alane, of Swords, County Dublin, he was two years in the seminary in June 1615.[473]

ROBERT TAYLOR (II) was ordained on 12 May 1680. In 1704, aged 46, he lived in Tobergregan, parish of Balmadum and Garristown, County Dublin; said Foundation masses, 1679–84.[474]

---

[465] LIS/4.   [466] Ibid; probably the same as James Talbot, below.   [467] LIS/7; G. da C., p. 262.   [468] Fenning, 1, p. 116.   [469] G. da C., pp 262, 432; LIS/4.   [470] LIS/4; G. da C., pp 262, 432.   [471] G. da C. op. cit., p. 432; Finegan, op. cit., p. 190.   [472] Fenning, 2, p. 75.   [473] Ibid., 1, p. 116; LIS/4, 7.   [474] *Register, 1704*; LIS/2, 4; Fenning, 2, p. 75.

THE STUDENTS

CHARLES THALLY was ordained on 6 January 1739.[475]

THOMAS, son of Robert, received minor orders on 19 December 1587.[476]

THOMAS, son of Gerald and Elena Marie, native of Cork, parish of St Robert, received the tonsure on 12 March 1588.[477]

JOHN TOBIN was ordained on 29 September 1664. In 1704 he lived in the city of Waterford, parish of St Peter, aged 62.[478]

RICHARD TOBIN was ordained on 12 March 1644.[479]

PATRICK TURNER died some time between 1590 and 1615.[480]

THOMAS TURNER, ordained in November 1629, had been a student in the college from 1623.[481]

VALOIS – See WALSH.

VALE – See WALSH.

VALERIO – See WALSH.

JOHN VATON was ordained on 6 January 1618.[482]

JOHN VERDON (I) received minor orders on 17 August 1676; became bishop of Ferns (1709–28). His doctorate was from the University of Évora.[483]

JOHN VERDON (II), was from Drogheda, diocese of Meath, and was ordained on 6 January 1687. In 1704, aged 41 years, he was living in Drogheda in St Peter's parish.[484]

VICENSE – See WHITE.

NICHOLAS VICENTE was three years in the seminary in June 1615.[485]

EDMUND VIN (WYNNE), a secular priest, returned to Ireland some time in 1615.[486]

VITUS – See WHITE.

NICHOLAS VOIS SJ (alias Lucher – Nicholas Luscher) was ordained on 4 April 1621.[487]

475 Fenning, 2, p. 76.   **476** Fenning, 2, p. 116.   **477** Ibid.   **478** Fenning, 2, p. 76; *Register, 1704*.   **479** Ibid. (1), p. 117.   **480** LIS/4.   **481** Ibid; G. da C., p. 262.   **482** LIS/7.   **483** Fenning, 2, p. 76; G. da C., p. 54.   **484** *Register, 1704*.   **485** LIS/4.   **486** Ibid.; G. da C., op. cit., p. 409.   **487** Fenning, 1, p. 117.

ALEXANDER VREUX (DEVEREUX) returned to Ireland some time between 1590 and 1615.[488]

JOHN WADDING returned to Ireland some time between 1590 and 1615.[489]

LUKE WADDING OFM, the renowned historian, theologian, founder/rector of the Irish College of St Isidore in Rome and annalist of the Franciscan Order, was a student of St Patrick's for about six months in 1610, before going on to Salamanca, Coimbra and Rome to complete his studies.[490]

MICHAEL WADDING SJ, from Waterford, studied at Irish College before entering the Society of Jesus in 1604. Also found as Miguel Godinez.[491]

PATRICK WALL (VALE), left the Irish college in 1592 for Valladolid, perhaps *en route* to the English College there. MacErlean cites a Patrick FitzRichard Wale.[492]

THOMAS WALL was ordained on 20 September 1614.[493]

EDMUND WALSH (VALESIO) received minor orders on 14 December 1666.[494]

JOHN WALSH died some time between 1590 and 1615.[495]

PATRICK WALSH (Vallois), received minor orders on 18 March 1641, was later a student at the University of Évora.[496]

THOMAS WALSH (Vallois), was a merchant in Lisbon for two years, before entering the Irish College as a collegian; he studied Humanities in the college and left in 1602 for Salamanca; he was ordained around the year 1615 and returned to Ireland. He became archbishop of Cashel in 1626, was hunted by the authorities, escaped to Spain, and died in Santiago de Compostela in 1654. Originally from Lismore diocese.[497]

DANIEL WARD was ordained on 11 March 1623.[498]

JOHN WATEO was ordained on 4 January 1618.[499]

JOHN WEEKES was ordained on 12 September 1740; his ordination was brought forward because of a dangerous sickness which demanded his immediate return to Ireland.[500]

---

488 LIS/4. **489** Ibid. **490** LIS/4; G. da C., p. 61, 407. **491** G. da C., p. 434. **492** LIS/4; G. da C. p. 409. **493** Fenning, 1, p. 117. **494** Fenning. 2, p. 76; LIS/4,7; MT 1666. **495** LIS/4. **496** LIS/7; G. da C., p. 53. **497** LIS/4; *Arch. Hib.*, ii (1914), p. 13; Brady, op. cit., ii pp 22-5. **498** LIS/7. **499** Fenning, 1, p. 117. **500** Fenning, 3, p. 158.

THE STUDENTS

ANDREW WHITE (VITTUS) received the tonsure and minor orders on 29 June 1671.[501]

FRANCIS WHITE SJ., born in Waterford on 16 March 1617, entered the Jesuit novitiate on 16 September 1634. He obtained an M.A., at the University of Coimbra and was a teacher of Greek, Hebrew and Moral Theology. He returned to Ireland in 1667 and died in Waterford in 1697.[502]

GEORGE WHITE was ordained on 27 December 1666.[503]

JOHN WHITE, son of Richard Vitus and Margarida Banes, native of Lisbon, living in the parish of St Paul, received the tonsure and minor orders on 21 December 1624.[504]

MATTHEW WHITE SJ, born 1550, received minor orders on 14 December 1666; he entered the Jesuits 1669, attended Évora college 1671, returned to Irish College 1675, from where he went to Funchal as a preacher. Six years later he was in Oporto and died 18 November 1700. He was a native of Clonmel.[505]

MICHAEL WHITE, from Meath, ordained on 12 October 1681, was appointed parish priest of Dunshaughlin, 1690.[506]

PATRICK WHITE son of Thomas and Bellina Wall, of Clonmel, diocese of Lismore, was ordained on 13 June 1609.[507]

STEPHEN 'Polyhistor' WHITE SJ, born Clonmel 1575, was one of the first three scholars at TCD and one of the first to enrol in Lisbon. He was world-famous in his time.[508]

RICHARD WHITE, son of Peter Vicense and Cecilia Berardan, was ordained on 11 March 1623.[509]

HENRY WISE was ordained on 20 December 1721.[510]

JAMES WISE died some time between 1590 and 1615.[511]

---

501 Fenning, 2, p. 76.   **502** LIS/4; G. da C., p. 433.   **503** Fenning, 2, p. 76.   **504** Fenning, 1, p. 117.   **505** Fenning, 2, p. 76; LIS/4,7.   **506** Fenning, 2, p. 76; *Register, 1704*.   **507** Fenning, 1, p. 117.   **508** Hogan, op. cit., pp 41–2; Finegan, op. cit., p. 211.   **509** Fenning, 1, p. 117.   **510** Fenning, 2, p. 76.   **511** LIS/4.

CHAPTER 6

The Earthquake of 1755, and Other Troubles

The patriarch of Lisbon proclaimed a public procession of penitence on 5 December 1755, in the aftermath of the earthquake. There was widespread acknowledgment of forecasts and prophecies, alluding to the terrible event and, certainly, there was a general belief that such a demonstration of public repentance was necessary.[1] Rose Macauley tells us of several eye-witness accounts of the survivors, notably that of Kitty Witham, a sister in the 'English Nunnery' in Lisbon, which was the Bridgettine convent of English nuns. Sister Catherine wrote a highly dramatic account to her mother in England on 27 January 1756.[2] 'The sisters ran to a low garden,' she relates, 'we layde under a pair tree, covered over with a Carpett, for eight days, I and some others being so vere frightened every time the wind blode the tree'; they then moved out into the open, they were so frightened. The royal family lived out of doors for a considerable time and thousands lost their lives, either buried in the ruined city or swept out to sea.

It was thought in Whitehall that Abraham Castres, the English envoy at Lisbon, had perished in the earthquake.[3] In December news was received that he was safe. The letters which passed between Castres and his close friend, Sir Benjamin Keene, ambassador at Madrid, are full of interesting and colourful sidelights on the aftermath of the earthquake, and private comments to him by Castres.

---

1 There are documents in the Biblioteca Nacional, Lisboa referring to prophecies and forcasts of the *terremoto*. There had been other earthquakes in Lisbon, for example, a serious one in 1344 and others from time to time. The reference to the procession of penitence is in *Códices e Maços, VIII, 1432–1511, No. 1478.f.8*. **2** *They went to Portugal* (London, 1946), pp 267–72. The nuns belonged to an order of contemplative sisters, who had fled to the continent from their abbey in England, Syon Abbey, after the Dissolution. They finally, after much wandering, settled in Lisbon in 1594. They stayed until 1861 but subsequently returned to England where they established themselves among the Dartmoor Hills. **3** Ibid. p. 277.

[100]

THE EARTHQUAKE OF 1755, AND OTHER TROUBLES

The English had very large business interests in Portugal for many centuries and also favourable treaties with Portugal. The Portuguese, on their voyages of discovery and commerce, had set up trading posts in the fifteenth century in the 'discovered' lands. These were called *Feitoria*, meaning a grouping of merchants living and trading abroad. The word was translated by the English traders in Portugal and its colonies as 'The Factory'. This meant for them the trading posts of *their* nationals, who lived and traded either in Portugal or in her possessions. The principal 'factories' were at Lisbon, Oporto and Madeira. They were like private clubs. The best-known was, perhaps, that in Oporto, based mainly on the port and wine trade; but the Lisbon factory was also important.[4]

Membership was based on the quantity of goods imported and on commercial and social reputation. The English consul was president of the Factory and it appears, that candidates for membership applied directly to him and he presented applicants to the members, who gave, or withheld, approval at their next meeting. Membership ensured very important and special protections and assistance for its members. They included a voice in decisions taken to facilitate the clearing of goods through customs; redressing anomalies in valuation of goods; drafting of new tariffs; and helping to secure space in the Custom House for landed goods, which was extremely important in Lisbon with the amount of overseas trade there.[5]

Factory membership was exclusively Protestant. Those elected were protected from prosecution by the Inquisition for heresy, through various agreements between Portugal and England. Irish Catholic merchants, who were, in theory, claimed as subjects of the English monarch, were expressly excluded.[6] Keene, who had been envoy to Lisbon for two years before he was appointed ambassador to Madrid, wrote to his friend, Castres, that he 'missed the jolly, free, Factory' people at the formal Madrid court, where the 'British merchants were mostly Irish Catholics'.[7]

One aspect of Castres' report, mentioned above, is of passing interest. It related to his dismissive remarks about some of the people who died in the earthquake. By the end of the year 1756, he sent home lists of the British dead, about seventy-eight altogether. 'Fortunately,' Rose Macauley

---

[4] See J.M.E. Shaw *The Anglo-Portuguese alliance and the English merchants in Portugal, 1654–1810* (Aldershot, 1998), pp 62–72. [5] Ibid. p. 62. [6] Ibid. p. 68; The relevant agreements concluded between the two powers were: in 1654 (Oliver Cromwell & João IV); 1661, the marriage treaty between Charles II and Catherine of Braganza; and the Methuen treaties of 1703. [7] Macauley, op. cit., p. 281.

reports him as indicating, 'it seemed that they did not all matter much: there were only two prominent members of The Factory ... and only two Englishwomen "of any note" among the dead'.[8] It appears, that, after the earthquake, the principal Factory families had secured their passages to England. Castres adds that, when he was less fatigued and troubled by his ordeal he would consider some way of putting 'the poorer sort' on to a Portuguese hulk or British vesse, until they could be shipped to England or Ireland He further reported that the 'Lisbon Irish,' who were 'extremely numerous, particularly of the poorer sort,' had suffered more heavily that the English and many of them were missing, but, in his opinion, it did not greatly matter, since most were 'so obscure as not to be known to any but the Irish friars'.[9] In fact, at least one Dominican friar had died in the disaster and untold numbers of poor Irish, who were eking out a living in the poorest and worst-hit areas of the city, also died.

After the earthquake the little-known and unsung hero of the restoration of the Irish College as an Irish seminary was Father Michael Daly. When the quake occurred there were eight students in St Patrick's College. Three are said to have returned to Ireland and the other five were sent, by royal decree, to the Colégio da Purificação, in the University of Évora, to pursue their course there until 1759,[10] so that their studies would not be interrupted. Michael Daly was one of these.

Three years later he returned to Lisbon to find that the college had been badly damaged in the earthquake but was still standing. It suffered its second disaster in 1759, when the Jesuits were suppressed and their property was taken over by the State. He was to dedicate himself, over the next twenty-one years, to the restoration of the College to the Irish.

He made strenuous efforts with the various monarchs, with government ministers, and influential people, to achieve his goal, and got many promises over the years, but no action until 30 April 1778, after the end of the Pombaline regime and the accession of the queen, Dona Maria, to the throne. Pombal's attitude to the Jesuits, which had become evident only after 1750, has been described by Boxer as 'a pathological hatred'; and he also states that 'his phobia had become the maniacal obsession which it remained for the rest of his life'.[11]

---

8 Ibid.　**9** Ibid. pp 278, 281.　**10** *IER*, McDonald, loc. cit., p. 311; a letter from the nunciature in Lisbon, in 1760, attests to these facts and also to the seizure of the college and property therein by order of the king: G. da C. op. cit., pp 380–3.
11 C.R. Boxer, op. cit., p. 186.

THE EARTHQUAKE OF 1755, AND OTHER TROUBLES

Father Daly was astonished to find that 'the plate, and ornaments, of our little church, which were so abundant, were given away by decrees from the late king [Dom José]; all our lands sold at public auction to different persons; a few houses which we possessed in this city, burnt in the earthquake; our other rents consisting in publick funds and royal grants in the most frightful confusion and some pensions on ecclesiastic Benefices to the yearly amount of about £200 English sterling, which the incumbants refuse to pay with various pretexts ... The house itself is very old, much hurted in the Earthquake, is now almost a ruin and would require an immense sum to repair it properly. Add to this a heavy debt against it for about £3,000, contracted in the time of the Jesuits.'[12] The college remained closed for many years and was reopened only through the persistence and efforts of this strong-minded Irish cleric. It continued to function until the Peninsular War caused a further closure in the early nineteenth century.

The Dominican father, Thomas Levin, rector of Corpo Santo, Lisbon, had told Father Michael Daly in 1780, that Dr John Thomas Troy, also a Dominican, and bishop of Ossory (1776–86), was 'desirous to know something of St Patrick's College, Lisbon'.[13] Thus began a correspondence, which lasted nearly nineteen years, between the bishop and Father Daly. Bishop Troy was to become one of the greatest champions of St Patrick's and his support and interest lasted all his life.

Father Daly had already been in correspondence with Dr Carpenter, archbishop of Dublin (1770–86), who had been ordained in Lisbon in 1752, and naturally took an interest in the fate of the Irish College there. In one of his letters to Troy, dated 1 September 1787, Father Daly writes, 'This house must be under obligation to your memory of it to the executors of the late Dr Carpenter.' The college did, in fact, receive some financial benefit from the deceased archbishop's estate, thanks to Dr Troy's intervention on its behalf. It would appear, that there were conditions 'that the money should be applied exclusively to the advantage of the diocese of Dublin'.[14] The detailed letters written by Father Daly give us insights into happenings at the college from 1780 to 1799. Unfortunately, the letters from Dr Carpenter and Dr Troy to the rector in Lisbon have not survived.

---

12 DDA File 117/7, letter Daly to Troy, 1 June 1780. **13** Ibid. **14** Ibid. letters same to same 1 Sept. 1787 & 9 May 1788. The executors were, in fact, his old friend, Father Bartholomew Sherlock, and Father Robert Bethel, PP at St Audeon's and vicar-general of Dublin. The archbishop left his gold-handed cane to the former and his silver snuff-box to the latter. See *Arch. Hib.* 4 (1915) 'Catholic episcopal wills' in the Public Record office, Dublin, William Carrigan pp 77–8.

Father Daly tells us in his letters that he came back to Lisbon on 18 March 1758, to find that the college had been confiscated by the government in the years immediately after the earthquake. He believed, that had any Irishman been on the spot, the confiscation would not have taken place. The college did not re-open until 1778, when Father Daly was nominated as rector, and a decree ordering the restoration of the college property was promulgated. Father Daly comments that the cardinal patriarch of Lisbon was then in possession of the college and that there would be difficulties in getting 'him out'. The college was designated nominally as a seminary for his own clergy by the cardinal. It appears that there were also problems with those who were then the owners of the land.[15]

Father Daly seems to have been a determined and tenacious man in spite of the frustrating treatment he received, and he ends his letter of 1 June 1780 on a somewhat optimistic note: 'I shall pursue the matter as far as I can and shall get such rents as I can, then take possession of the house.' He nonetheless points out, 'I am heartily tired of the job. I have sacrificed to it the best years of my life, my country, my connections and, in fine, everything that is dear to man; and for some time past my presence would be very necessary in Dublin for family reasons; in the meantime I cannot sufficiently praise and admire the providence of God, who has furnished me with the means of supporting this expensive business,[16] which I have cheerfully done unaided by any concurrence from any quarter and if I can bring it to any advantageous conclusion, Ireland will reap the profits without contributing a farthing.' He worked tirelessly from the late 1750s to 1778 for the return of the college. He protests that he did this tedious business supported alone by the ardent desire of serving 'my Religion and country'.[17] He also describes himself as being of a sanguine nature, which is, perhaps, a gross understatement. It is interesting to note that he visited Dublin early in 1774. He wrote from there to the archbishop of Lisbon, Dom Francisco de Saldanha, telling him that he would be leaving for Portugal at the end of May. He explains that he is occupied in Dublin with family matters and points out to the archbishop that it would be a great act of charity if His Grace would interest himself in the restoration of the Irish College, which had ceased for fifteen years to help '*aquela aflita missao*'.[18]

15 Ibid. letter same to same, 1 June 1780. **16** This is probably an oblique reference to the pension he received, as emeritus professor of Greek, from his employment in the College of the Nobles. **17** DDA same to same, 1 June 1780. **18** Translation:

THE EARTHQUAKE OF 1755, AND OTHER TROUBLES

He was well-acquainted with an eminent humanist and professor of Greek in Lisbon, Father José de Oliveira, the 'P. Custodio,' mentioned by Father Daly as having written to him in Dublin in 1774, telling him that he should get in touch with Archbishop Saldanha of Lisbon.[19] He was, of course, a close friend of Father Bartholomew Sherlock, parish priest of St Catherine's in Meath Street, Dublin, from their days in the seminary of St Patrick, Lisbon and at the University of Évora. In one of his letters to Dr Troy he mentions that he has not heard from this friend for some time. They did, in fact, correspond throughout their lives.[20] One may safely assume that they met over the years, possibly, during Father Daly's visit in 1774. In addition, Daly was a lifelong friend of another classical scholar, Dr William Bermingham, professor of Greek in Coimbra University and later official visitor to the Irish Colleges in Spain and rector of the Irish College, Salamanca (1778–80).[21]

Father Daly was a Dublin secular priest, a classical scholar and an able canonist. Apart from Portuguese, he spoke fluent French and German. When he finished his studies, Pombal invited him to accept the professorship of Greek in the College of the Nobles, *o Colégio dos Nobres*, recently founded. This was a very prestigious position and, as Pombal had closed down the Irish College, Daly accepted. He constantly reminded Pombal of his determination to get back the Irish College. Luckily for him he received a pension, as emeritus professor, from this college for the rest of his life. A shortage of professors of Greek, and indeed other subjects, was one of the direct consequences of the suppression of the Jesuits at that time.

The final letter from Fr Daly is dated 22 January 1799. He died five years later.

Dr Bartholomew Crotty, who succeeded Fr Daly as rector, continued to report on the college to Dr Troy. Other Irish priests, resident in Lisbon, also corresponded with Dr Troy until 1822. These were Fathers Joseph Joy Deane, William Sherry and John Dunn. There is also an interesting letter to the archbishop from a student-priest, Francis Archer, in 1807.[22] Dr Troy died, on 11 May 1823, at the advanced age of 84. The Peninsular War, 1808–13, was the next major disruption in the life of St Patrick's. Despite the best efforts of another trio of determined priests the college finally

---

'that afflicted Irish Mission'; G. da C., p. 385. **19** Ibid. **20** DDA, letter, 18 April 1795, Daly to Troy: 'Besides yourself he is almost the only one in Ireland I correspond with.' **21** McDonald, loc. cit., p. 311. **22** The correspondence of the priests and student will be examined in Chapter 7 on the last years of the college.

closed in 1834.[23] Under the terms of its foundation if it ceased to exist, its assets were to pass to the Irish Dominican Fathers in Corpo Santo.

After its closure in 1834, and following nearly eighty years of unrest in Portugal, the college finally became the property of the State when a republic was proclaimed in 1910. It is now a municipal courthouse. It is worth, noting that in recent years the building has been sensitively restored, and when a plaque was placed on it some years ago, commemorating its Irish connection, our diplomatic mission and the Irish community in Lisbon celebrated the event in style. When I first visited the house in late 1998 it was a bustling busy place.[24]

THE CHAPEL

The most significant features of the restored building were the few remains of the former chapel. In some of the manuscripts inspected the beauty of the chapel is frequently mentioned and former students lamented its decay and its ruinous state after the earthquake. The chapel was notable for its fine decoration. Even after the ravages of the earthquake it had been restored to some semblance of its former beauty, as may be gleaned from the account of the three concerned clerics in 1822, to be examined in the next chapter. In one of the descriptions of the chapel, in a contemporary document dated 1680 and seen by one of the nineteenth-century Irish Jesuit transcribers of manuscript material in Portugal, there was apparently a vivid description of the newly adorned St Patrick's chapel. Unfortunately, he did not transcribe this description.[25]

However, Gonçalves da Costa comes to our rescue once again. He gives us a description, albeit brief, by Carvalho da Costa, found in an eighteenth-century account:

> ... pequena, de uma so nave, com a porta principal voltada a sul. Ao centro do retábulo do altar-mor, imagen de Nossa Senhora dos

[23] DDA. Three other priests from three different dioceses wrote a very strong and concerned letter on the state of the college, to Dr Troy in 1822, which will also be discussed in Chapter 7.   [24] My visit was arranged through the good offices of the Irish embassy in Lisbon, and I was shown over the building by Dra. Maria Celia Pereira, who pointed out the many remaining features of the old seminary and the fine views of the river Tagus and estuary to be had from some of the courtrooms on the upper floors.   [25] LIS/4.

THE EARTHQUAKE OF 1755, AND OTHER TROUBLES

Remédios, orago, e nos quatro nichos laterais as imagens dos santos Inacio de Loiola, Francisco Xavier, Francisco de Borja e Luís Gonzaga. Ha tres capelas laterais, duas delas do lado do Evangelho, a saber: de São Patrício, com altar privilegiado, e a de São João Baptista, no qual se guardam diversas relíquias e dois braços, um de prata e outro de pau pintado.[26]

Another benefactor of the chapel was Dom Luís Fernandes de Almada together with his wife, Dona Isabel Gomez. Dom Luís bequeathed a large sum of money, *cem mil rs de juro en cada hum ano perpetuos* (100,000 *reis* in an annuity in perpetuity), for work on the church and its maintenance. A contract to this effect was drawn up on 1 June 1620, between the donor and the college; it also specified that he should be buried there when the chapel was completed.[27] It was laid down that the *capella de São Patrício*, chapel of St Patrick, was to be made *muita fermosa*, very beautiful, and the bones of his first wife, Isabel Gomez, were to be transferred there from her resting place in the São Roque church when the chapel was completed. Instructions were given in the contract also that a very fine *retábulo*, altarpiece, with the image of St Patrick in its centre was to be installed and ornamentation was to be of silver.[28] Decently adorned sepulchres were to be installed with two inscriptions, one in Latin and the other in Portuguese.

Provision was made also that two Masses were to be said daily for the repose of the souls of Luís de Almada and of his first wife. Dom Luis died on 26 July 1620, Isabel on 16 January 1610, before the acquisition of the final college site. His second wife, Dona Cecilia de Lega, was also a benefactor of the college. She donated to it the Charneca farm, with vine and olive groves, in Varatejo. She was an Irishwoman, was forty years of

---

26 G. da C., p. 441. Translation: ' ... small, with a single nave, and a main door, facing south. In the centre of the high altar, there is an image of Our Lady of Succour and in the four side niches the images of saints Ignatius Loyola, Francis Xavier, Francis Borgia and Louis Gonzaga. There are three side chapels, two of them on the Evangelist's side, that is, St Patrick, with a privileged altar and St John the Baptist, in which are kept different relics and two arms, one of silver and the other of painted wood.' **27** LIS/4. **28** When one sees the magnificence of the high altar, with its silver ornamentation, in the Irish Dominican Sisters' convent of Bom Successo, Belem, it is easy to imagine the beauty of that of St Patrick's chapel, also from the same era. Both would have been the products of contemporary Portuguese style and craftmanship.

age in 1631, and died childless in 1663. She herself had, apparently, lived in the Charneca *quinta* which she left to the Irish College.[29] Dona Cecilia also left a legacy to St Patrick's College for the setting up of a chapel in the college church, dedicated to St John the Baptist, with a '*dotação suficiente para uma missa diária por alma das duas*'.[30]

When I visited the former chapel in 1998, it was gratifying to see that the wishes of the generous benefactors of the chapel of St Patrick in the Irish College, Lisbon, had, indeed been carried out to the letter. It was of particular interest to discover that two tablets, one in Latin and the other in Portuguese, were retained. Not only did they testify to the transfer of the bones of both Isabel Gomez and her husband, Dom Luís, on 8 August 1680, but they paid tribute to them as *insignes bemfeitores*, eminent benefactors, of the seminary, who, with great piety and zeal, contributed to the education of so many Irish students for the priesthood. The General of the Jesuit Order in Rome, Oliva, commented on the completion of the chapel in letters in 1680 and mentioned that the remains were brought to the newly-completed chapel and solemn High Mass was celebrated.[31]

The only remaining feature of the original chapel, apart from the tablets mentioned, is a fragment of painting on the ceiling over what was the high altar. This decoration is a painting in the shape of a medallion of two hearts, side by side, one encircled with the crown of thorns, the other with a garland of flowers, and surrounded by five cherubs. It appears to be in honour of the devotion to the two Sacred Hearts of Jesus and Mary. In the ceiling decoration it appears that the two devotions are combined.[32] Though not documented this decoration probably dates from the late 18th century.

DISTURBANCES

Life in the college from 1590 to 1624 was, relatively, quiet and serene. There was major unrest in 1624 with the imposition of Portuguese

---

29 G. da C., p. 274; idem, 'St Patricks school' pp 46–7, 49 & 50; because she had no descendants, D. Cecilia was able to declare the students of St Patrick's her heirs to various properties: G. da C., p. 271. **30** Translation: 'a donation for a daily mass for the souls of the two of us [herself and her sister]'. Sister Juana da Cruz, deceased, who had been a nun in the convent of St Monica was the sister of D. Cecilia. G. da C., p. 271. **31** MT 26 Aug. 1680 & 21 Oct. 1680.

rectors.³³ This gave rise to some unseemly behaviour, such as the peremptory ejection of the visiting Jesuit father, already described, and this disorder continued, resulting in the dismissal of Cornelio da Rocha. Whether he was accused of fomenting the disorder or some complicity in it, or of being merely unable to quell it, is not altogether clear. From time to time after 1624 there were rumblings of discontent about the courses of study. Complaints of this kind surfaced at regular intervals. There was, usually, a stock reply from the General of the Jesuits, promising to look into the matter, or else a quiet rebuke, telling the student to submit details of his dissatisfaction to the Portuguese provincial. In 1690 Patrick Dowdall, Andrew Mathews and Michael Greames complained to the General in Rome about the Theology course.³⁴ However, the General gave some timely advice to Andrew Mathews: he exhorted him to study simplicity and peace, with a gentle reminder that juniors in Theology are not in a position to judge of the utility or uselessness of *Hiatus (Dictati)*. That is for the masters to decide.³⁵

In November 1689, Edward Murphy, shortly after his arrival in St Patrick's, suggested to the General in Rome that the students should be allowed to preach 'domestic sermons' as an exercise and got quite a sympathetic letter in reply. However, the General was somewhat irritated at a later date about receiving a letter from the same student marked *'soli'*, the equivalent of 'private and confidential'; and which was reserved for matters of the greatest secrecy.³⁶

There were also, at times, complaints about the food served in the refectory or other 'domestic' grievances. There was, for instance, one revolt among the collegians who described the food as 'fit only for dogs'. In 1688 the General, Thyrsus Gonzalez, remonstrated with collegians who had

---

32 The special devotion to the Sacred Heart of Jesus was formally instituted by Sister Margaret Mary Alacoque (1647–90). This devotion became widely popular at that time and was favoured by the Jesuits. It was not until 1765 that several churches were permitted to celebrate the feast by Clement XIII. The permission was extended to the whole church in 1856. Blessed John Eudes, founder of the Eudist order in France, born in Normandy in 1601, died in 1680, propagated the devotion to the Immaculate Heart of Mary and the celebration of the feast was permitted in 1855 by Pius IX. See W.E. Addis and T. Arnold, *A Catholic dictionary* (London, 1917), pp 401–2. **33** This had resulted in a memorial, in Latin, being sent to the Father General in Rome by concerned students, and signed by twenty-one of them. See G. da C., p. 412. **34** MT 15 Apr. 1690: 8 and 22 July 1690. **35** MT 8 July 1690. **36** MT 11 Apr. 1693.

complained to their rector about badly cooked food by showing him the offending portions. He regarded the behaviour as neither gracious nor courteous. In an incident nine years earlier, in 1679, the General, Father Oliva, had been horrified by the students' rude behaviour concerning a complaint of this sort. In a strong letter to them he makes his point of view clear in no uncertain manner. Having carried out an investigation he found no grounds for complaints about the bread 'which was of the same quality as in the Scottish College and other seminaries in Rome'. He conceded that, on one or two days only, the wine began to go bad and there was no possibility at the time of a replacement. He adds, 'in all my nineteen years of rule I have never received such a complaint'. He pointedly reminded them that 'in the Roman seminary there are many nobles paying for their keep, and in the other colleges, especially the German colleges, where the flower of the nobility are'. His advice to the complaining Irish students was to follow their example ... [37]

Another bone of contention with the students was the admission of boarders to the college. Father Oliva instructed the rector in Lisbon, Francisco Caldeyra, on 7 July 1680, not to admit boarders, because of the detrimental effect on studies and the displeasure it occasioned among the *alumni*.[38]

A practice which caused friction between the rectors and the students was the issuing of letters in Ireland, which were found to be false as regards age. Caldeyra writing in August 1680, tells Oliva that, in a recent case, Nicholas Stafford was ordained on the strength of letters patent brought by him. As Stafford was not aware of the false entry of his age, he was not expelled and, although he celebrated mass twice, he was 'now abstaining from doing so'. The rector mentions another student Peter Dillon, whose date of birth was falsified. He was also about to be ordained.[39]

The rector lays the blame squarely with the students and the Jesuits in Ireland and tells the General that in order to enter the seminary the students feign the age necessary under Canon Law. After they have been admitted, they do not fear to be expelled. Caldeyra recommends that the Irish Fathers should be warned to be more cautious about giving letters-patent and that, in future, anyone bringing false letters should be expelled. In 1681 Oliva put in operation measures to provide against unsuitable and under age candidates being sent to Lisbon.[40]

---

37 MT 15 May 1688; 13 Nov. 1679.   **38** MT 7 July 1680.   **39** MT 26 Aug. 1680.
40 MT 4 Jan. 1681.

THE EARTHQUAKE OF 1755, AND OTHER TROUBLES

Another letter was sent in 1683 by the General, Carlos Noyelle, to the students of the Irish seminary in response to their suggestions about the management of the college. He is sympathetic to those complaints, which touch on their comfort and peace, but warns them not to meddle in other matters, which concern the government of the college.[41] There are many other letters regarding problems of discipline at the college and the advice of Noyelle to Manuel Soares, rector, 1682–6, is 'to keep the students to their duty and exhort them to join Christian piety with study – but *suaviter et strene*'![42]

Complaints from the students about rectors surfaced once in a while. These were made to the General, to the provincial in Lisbon, or even to the papal nuncio; but not all complaints came from the students. Staff members also showed concern for discipline and often for what they regarded as laxity. Noyelle in 1684, a year after his earlier words of advice to him on discipline, had complaints about the rector, Soares. In these cases the General wrote to the provincial to deal with the matter. Soares was accused of giving leave easily for walks, rarely presiding at meals, allowing the students without any acccompanying Jesuit to go into town, overlooking breaches of silence, not listening to the *consultores* and not showing them the accounts each month, as is the custom in that province. The General tells the provincial he is dismayed that the rector rules so despotically and does not listen to the *consultores* who, as their name suggests, were meant to be consulted.

A year later practically the same complaints turn up, and once again the General writes to the provincial. This time the criticism is even stronger. The superiors are not looking after the students, there are no visits to them during prayer, and exhortations; and disputations, which should be held each week, are hardly held in the whole year. He further states that several of the theologians do not take notes to lectures, and even on Christmas Day the rector does not preside at the students' meals. The minister also follows the rector's example. The priests, who live in the seminary, leave the house in the morning or on feast days to hear confessions of women in their own homes. This happens when 'our own church is full and there is no one to hear confessions'. He further asserts that the rector leaves the house, when the other priests are out and there is no one to attend to sick-calls, which are frequently made. He suggests that all this happens in spite of his admonitions, and he considers that the provincial must look around

41 MT 8 Sept. 1683.   42 MT 3 Dec. 1683.

for a new rector who will zealously do his duty by the students. However, he puts decisive action on the long finger and leaves the situation as it is, with the lame excuse that, as Rector Soares is nearly finished his three-year term it would be advisable to seek names for a new appointment in good time.[43]

The most serious disturbance in St Patrick's College was sparked off by Dionisio Charti (Denis Carthy), described as a born agitator, who took up the cudgels in the 1690s against the rector, Francisco Tavares (1692–5). The row erupted over the removal of a 'pro-Irish rector', Afonso de Mexia (1600–92), and the appointment of Tavares. Afonso de Mexia had already been rebuked for his unorthodox methods.[44] Although initially the complaint was against the new rector, it flared into a serious outbreak of violence. On 28 November 1692, Denis Carthy wrote to the General of the Society in Rome, Father Thyrsus Gonzalez. Carthy was rebuked by the General and told to submit his criticisms to the Portuguese provincial. Carthy was supported by several of the collegians, including John Corkran, Edward Murphy, James Cusack and Nicholas Carbery. This revolt obviously was building up for some time.

Gonçalves da Costa tells us that Denis Carthy was astute, an agitator and opportunist. He had been in the college for five years and showed little application to study. Considering him incorrigible, the rector, Sebastião de Magalhães, expelled him in 1692. He was re-instated when he promised to amend his ways. Apparently, with the connivance of an influential ally, D. António Jorge de Melo, heir of the college benefactor, D. António Fernandes Ximenes, and other students, he engaged in all sorts of mischief, such as stealing the ledgers from the rector's office and causing uproar in the college. The rector called in outside help and Carthy was apprehended. His influential friend had him released. The matter went to law, with decrees, appeals and counter-appeals. Even the under-secretary of state, Mendes Foios, was a supporter of Carthy. In the end the expulsion was upheld.[45]

Nine years later a minor infringement of a college regulation caused fisticuffs and recriminations between a collegian and a Portuguese lay-brother, who was acting as porter. Edward Higgins without permission

---

[43] MT 8 Apr. 1684 and 19 May 1685. [44] The General told de Mexia, that he had hoped that controversies and recrimination which seemed to follow him were at an end, but he had to transfer him to another house in Lisbon: MT 17 Jan. 1693.
[45] G. da C., 'St Patrick's school', pp 41–4.

sent a boy to collect the post, as he was expecting an important letter. The gatekeeper, when the boy returned with the mail, took the letters from him and sent them, with Higgins, to the vice-principal. One thing led to another and the proctor, who had also intervened, accused Higgins of stealing and refused to give him a letter addressed to him. At this point, all hell broke loose. Accusations were exchanged and the priest withdrew, but Higgins continued to rant and rave and others who tried to intervene became involved in fisticuffs between brothers and students. The matter was finally resolved with the conclusion of a board of inquiry, that the incident was due to the angered state of the brother and the discourteous, rude and presumptuous behaviour of Higgins. Other students who joined in the melee, were rude and indominable and treated the priests with lack of courtesy. There were apologies all round and the matter ended there.[46]

Finally, the admission or non-admission of candidates for vacant places was a continuous bone of contention and dissatisfaction. On 30 November 1694, Father John Higgins SJ when about to return to Ireland at the request of the Superior of the Jesuit Order in Ireland, Thomas Eustace, wrote him a letter in which he criticized the running of St Patrick's College by Rector Tavares:[47]

> ... there being of late two places vacant, came one Patrick Cary, of Dublin, a priest with a patent from Father Anthony Knoles [a former Superior of the Jesuits in Ireland], but the rector of the seminary alleging that the year was scarce would not receive him and, in the meantime received, one Keating who neither had Patent from the mission nor came hither with intention to enter the seminary, but finding friends to intercede for him he entered and Father Cary, that had more right remained abroad ... In the seminary, within a year and a half will be eight places vacant; two are already ordained for Thomas and Laurence Gibbons, nephews of Father James Gibbons [SJ, and a Dubliner], another young man is studying in Évora called Daniel Keohane, worthy of a place and expecting it ...

Father Hennesssy, a later superior of the Jesuits in Ireland, also complained to the General, Francisco Retz, in 1736, on the score of the

---

46 Ibid. pp 44–5.   **47** LIS/4. Father John Higgins SJ lived in the city of Waterford, aged 48 years, in 1704, parish of St Olaf and was Ordinary in 1689.

provincial in Lisbon admitting two youths to the college without Hennessy's knowledge; which made it impossible for him to keep his promise to the archbishops of Tuam and Cashel. Hennessy threatened to go to the Sacred Congregation about the matter.[48]

There are examples of disputes and disturbances in all the Irish colleges. Some were about trivial matters, others of a more serious nature. One, which caused a great deal of upheaval, resulting in the expulsion of four students, was what seems at this remove to have been simply a matter of flouting of the authority of a rector, in a matter of simple charity. It happened in the Irish College, Salamanca. A poor, itinerant Irish tailor came to the college looking for work and some of the students asked if he could be employed to make clothing for them, to be paid for with their *viaticum*. The rector refused, saying that they could not take in an unknown stranger just like that. In defiance of the rector's orders some of the students took him in, hid him and fed him against the express orders of the rector. When they were found out there was Hell to pay. Dr Patrick Curtis, who was rector of St Patrick's Salamanca, and later primate at Armagh, had experienced major disorder at the college over this matter.[49] In November 1790, and again in February, he sent some bulky packages of documents regarding the trouble at his college to Father Michael Daly for transmission to Dr Troy. These were send back to Dublin by Father Daly in the care of a Dr Donnellan, a Dublin physician, who had come to Lisbon to accompany a sick man in his care, and was returning to his practice in 88 Dame Street in 1791, promising faithfully to deliver the package to the Archbishop of Dublin.[50] Father Daly, in the accompanying letter, says that in his own experience, 'with respect to this house the collegians have ever lived in peace, and have always treated me with respect and every demonstration of obedience. I never had anything to complain of on that head. Whatever heart-burns I received here, I received them from those, from whom it should not be expected, and I can with a safe conscience assert, that I never gave them cause. But peace to all such!' A truly remarkable man, who ruled the Irish College in Lisbon, with wisdom, benevolence and success, over almost his whole life, devoted to the service of the college he loved so well and saved from oblivion.[51]

Register, 1704. **48** MT 19 Nov. 1736. **49** See Sal. Archs., *legajo* II/ 6, 7, 8 for an account of this unhappy incident. **50** DDA, letter Daly to Troy, 23 Feb. 1791. **51** Ibid. same to same, 2 Feb. 1792.

CHAPTER 7

The Last Years

During the life-span of the Irish College of St Patrick, Lisbon, was certainly, from the contemporary accounts, the centre and hub of activities of all kinds. It was at the crossroads of East and West. The far-flung Portuguese colonies and overseas possessions made it not only the purveyor of the exotic products of the Orient, Africa and the New World,[1] but was also the melting-pot of the people and cultures of this ultramarine empire. Over the centuries it was the microcosm and counting-house of a newly opened-up world, a centre of political intrigue, religious feuds, military intervention, the theatre of wars with wider interests than just those of the kingdom of Portugal. It attracted the idle rich and the poorest of the poor – tradesmen, factors, intellectuals, scholars, dilettantes, invalids, the greedy, the idealists, the devout, the austere, the frivolous, the zealots, heretics, confessors, admirals, Crusaders, freebooters, Freemasons, Liberals, soldiers, slaves, generals,tracterians, Bible-vendors and English, Scots, French, Spanish, Jews, Irish, Italians and Germans. All human life was there, to borrow a modern phrase.

Lisbon was variously described as beautiful, elegant, exotic and filthy, noisy and dangerous. The books about Lisbon, and Portugal, are legion. No capital, and its surrounding countryside, has been described by so many writers. The beauty of the city is proverbial; its location at the mouth of the Tagus is spectacular, with a backdrop of hills, which enhance its magnificent setting, as its elegant streets, squares, parks and gardens slope down to the water's edge. Its intrinsic beauty has attracted travellers from many lands over the centuries. In particular the intrepid English travellers of the eighteenth century were drawn to the Portuguese capital. Many of them published books about Lisbon, and indeed the country in general, in such numbers that one might be excused for thinking that they travelled nowhere else. Lord Byron, Henry Fielding, William Beckford, Robert Southey, George Borrow were a few of the Portuguese capital's

1 Sugar, spices, pepper, mace, nutmegs, cloves, cotton, silk, porcelain, gold, silver, diamonds. See Boxer, op. cit., pp 51–64.

famous visitors, who wrote – not always favourably – about this great city with its toes almost in the Atlantic Ocean.

Many Irish, too, found their way to Lisbon; not, however, of the rich and famous variety. They were mostly clerics, students, merchants and soldiers, many fleeing from religious persecution at home. Perhaps one of the most intriguing is the shadowy figure of Francis Bermingham, a mysterious young man, who was a student for the priesthood in the Irish College, Salamanca from 1745 to 1747. He left there under a cloud to return to Ireland and died in 1749 in Jamaica, 'whither his father who did not wish to keep him in his house in Dalgan, in the diocese of Tuam, sent him'. His connection with Lisbon is a somewhat tenuous one. Instead of embarking for Ireland from Bilbao or a French port he chose to travel overland to Lisbon, and spent nearly two weeks there before leaving on 2 March 1747, for the sea journey to Dublin. In a letter to the rector of Salamanca, John O'Brien, he wrote on 21 February 1747, 'there is a ship bound for Dublin but I am not sure when she will depart. My lodging and victualling here, a footy[2] dinner and more footy supper, costs me 8 *reals* a day *sine ullo remedio*. To be sure Lisbon is the most wicked hole in the world, it is abominable to relate its actions, customs and manners.'[3]

THE PENINSULAR WAR

'We hope here for peace and yet every preparation is for war' (Michael Daly, 1797).

The nineteenth century brought new political problems for the ailing Irish College in Lisbon. In the wake of the French Revolution and the new political theories and philosophies which were spreading everywhere, nervous European monarchs and their governments sought to align themselves against France. Portugal had traditionally allied herself with Britain but tried hard to maintain a neutral position with France and Spain. Events quickly overtook Portugal, as French armies of invasion spread out over Europe, and Britain blockaded the continent. The Iberian peninsula became the theatre of a six-year war, as France and Britain, in the main, battled it out on many fronts.

2 (Obsolete) mean.   **3** *Salamanca letters*, 13 AA I 74.

THE LAST YEARS

The British had, at the beginning of the conflict, blockaded the entrance to the Mediterranean, with the help of the Portuguese, and eventually extended this to the whole continent. The French, in turn, blockaded shipping in and out of Britain and Ireland. As far as the Irish were concerned, travel and post were restricted. As the war went on for six years it created many worries for the students and staff of the college. The French, under General Junot, invaded Portugal in 1807, and occupied Lisbon on 30 November of that year. The kingdom was the arena of battle, until the French finally pulled out in May 1813. Life must have been very difficult for the exiled seminarians and their professors, with the college virtually closed down for the duration of the war. Communication by post was greatly restricted and convoys had to be awaited to travel back and forth to Ireland. In times of war grants from the royal purse were held up and went into arrears, so that the straitened financial position must have been even more precarious than usual. Michael Daly was very apprehensive about the threat of war because he knew from experience the consequences to public credit and particularly in relation to St Patrick's. The college depended for its income on royal funds and charities. In 1795 these amounted to £200 per year. He knew that it was 'a system in this country to pay one [moiety?] and the other extremely ill, whenever they are engaged in war. Thus I have not yet recovered the first of the year 1792, nor the last of this year and a half ... I hope the war will be soon over and then we probably shall recover readily.'[4]

The prince regent, the royal family and the court left for Brazil just before the invasion in 1807. Saraiva tells us that '10,000 people embarked on a fleet of all the seaworthy ships that could be assembled in the Tagus estuary, and sailed for Brazil'.[5] Among these was an Irish priest, Father Hyacinth Joyce, who later, on his return, became rector of the College of St Patrick. He travelled to Brazil in the suite of a Portuguese nobleman as chaplain to his household.[6]

In 1808 there was a popular revolt against the French. The British sent in a military force under the command of Arthur Wellesley, a Dublinman and later duke of Wellington, who occupied the city, when the French withdrew. The war dragged on until 1813, and then another Irishman, William Beresford, also in the British service, became a kind of viceroy of Portugal. Various political upheavals occurred, culminating in a

4 DDA, letters Daly to Troy 6 July 1797 and 4 Dec. 1795. **5** Op. cit., p. 88.
6 See details of Father Joyce later in this chapter.

constitutional assembly. Differences of opinion regarding the Constitution surfaced and in 1821 the *Cortes* recalled Dom João VI, now king, from Brazil. He returned, but his heir, Pedro IV, refused to leave his adopted country and was proclaimed emperor of Brazil, which became an independent kingdom. When João VI died in 1826, his son, the emperor, refused the crown of Portugal and abdicated in favour of his daughter, D. Maria da Glória, then aged seven years.[7]

The story of the last years of the Irish College is not a happy one. After the death of the rector, Michael Daly,[8] things went from bad to worse, and the college went steadily downhill after the re-opening at the end of the Peninsular War. The successor to Father Daly was Dr Bartholomew Crotty, who ran the college for twelve years. I found very little information about his administration. However, under his governance studies for the priesthood continued apace, three professors were employed to conduct the courses, and there were nine students, and four servants. All were fully supported, 'as were doctors, apothecaries and washing bills. On his succession he found a well-stored college coffer. This respectable state continued for four or five years before decline set in'.[9]

For the last years of the history of the Irish College, Lisbon I have had to rely on scant documentary evidence. Since Michael Daly was from the archdiocese of Dublin and his extant correspondence is almost wholly that which he wrote to Archbishop Troy, the emphasis is, of necesssity almost entirely devoted to that part of the country. Names of priests and students crop up in the correspondence, often without the relevant information as to whether these are of staff or students. I propose to present this incomplete material, just as it relates to such individuals, in the hope that others may take up their stories at another stage, so that we may get a complete picture of those students, who attended the college in its last days.

FRANCIS ARCHER was a student-priest from the diocese of Dublin. He came to Lisbon in 1807; he tells Dr Troy in a letter dated 20 September 1807,[10] that his journey took twenty days. It appears that he formed a very

---

7 Saraiva, op. cit., pp 93 & 95.   **8** Father Daly, as we have noted, had succeeded in getting the college re-started under great difficulties and governed it wisely for twenty-one years, with its income slowly returning to normal and collegians beginning to filter in again from Ireland.   **9** DDA, from the letter to Dr Troy, in 1822, from the three concerned priests. This is treated later in this chapter.   **10** Ibid. letter Archer to Troy, 20 Sept. 1807.

bad impression of the college and shows concern about the course of study he is supposed to follow and the state of discipline within the institution. Several of the other students at the time were 'externs' from the north of Ireland. They came to commence Philosophy and there was no professor in the house to teach them. He asks the archbishop to recommend him to the Irish College in Rome. French troops, he says, are daily expected and he fears that the students will be sent home. 'The Prince is determined on retiring to the Brazils, should his affairs take an unfavourable turn. All the convents and churches have already received orders for the securing of their plate. The Portuguese have now nearly collected together all the ships of war; and ships' carpenters and all other workmen of that description work night and day in fitting-out vessels to carry off, should circumstances demand, the property of the inhabitants.'[11]

MR BARRON came to the college in May 1830.[12]

MR BURNE.[13]

PAUL BYRNE, from Dublin, arrived in Lisbon around 22 July 1791. When he finished his course he stayed on to teach Philosophy. He had left for Dublin, on a ship bound for Liverpool, on 6 July 1797. Daly reports to the archbishop that 'he always behaved well' while living at the college.[14]

JOHN COYNE, from the diocese of Armagh, finished his course as a collegian and stayed on as a professor. He left for home in 1797; described by the rector as 'a man of great modesty, piety and diligence in the discharge of his duties'.[15]

BARTHOLOMEW CROTTY had a distinguished career; he was rector of the Irish College, Lisbon, from 1799 to 1811, and subsequently president of St Patrick's College, Maynooth (1813–33) and for the last thirteen years of his life served as bishop of Cloyne (1833–46). He did not have an easy life in Lisbon. Having taken over when the college was going into a decline, he experienced the French occupation of the city, the flight of the royal family

---

11 Ibid. **12** IDA, E. 9 –'Joyce's Diary'. This diary, which is in the Irish Dominican Archives, and which I refer to as Joyce's Diary, is a rather scattered notebook belonging to the rector, Dr Hyacinth Joyce, with cryptic entries, often just a name, sometimes a date. **13** Ibid. no details. Other names found, without details, apart from Mr Burne are Diego Carlos Duff, Geraldo Gould, D. Moran and Mr Walsh. **14** DDA, letter, Daly to Troy, 22 July 1791. **15** Ibid. letter, same to same, 6 July 1797.

to Brazil, and the turbulent years of the war period. His problems were manifold. The college was closed for a long period and the payments for the upkeep were well in arrears; in fact, he states in 1804,[16] that he has not been able to get arrears going back to before Michael Daly's death. In the same year he lost two of the stalwarts of the teaching staff, Messrs Mullan and Redmond, a heavy blow to him as, since taking office, he tells us that he 'had little else to support me than the friendly counsels and cordial co-operation of these two gentlemen'.[17]

He has bitter words to say, *vis-à-vis* the conditions in the college, about the bishops of Ireland, with only one or two exceptions: 'I have seen the Bishops of Ireland ... much more indifferent to our well, or ill-being, than they should be were the establishment destined for the propagation of Christianity in North America or Botany Bay.'[18] Nor does he spare the Portuguese government for 'their bad faith and poverty' in their dealings with him and his college. He feels strongly that, as he is unable, because of the narrowness of his circumstances, to advance the interests of the college, and is defenceless against the insinuations and open attacks on his administration, he should resign as soon as he can with honour. This was not to be for some years.

JOSEPH JOY DEANE: the only item regarding this cleric is a letter, which he wrote to Dr Troy in 1807.[19] It is a letter of recommendation for Father Lennon, who studied in the college as an extern, and asks for the archbishop's protection for Lennon 'during his stay in Dublin'. Deane had some financial difficulties due to 'a plan' in which he had the assistance of numerous noblemen and the nuncio. It appears that his difficulties were due to the death of the minister, the count of Vila Verde. There was a project afoot to set up a school for day-pupils. A petition from St Patrick's to obtain a licence to take in paying pupils to be instructed in *Religion, Letras e Linguas* was lodged, in fact, in 1804 and approved by the count of Vila Verde. An advertisement regarding the plan appeared in the *Gazeta de Lisboa* on 4 December 1804.[20] Father Deane returned to Dublin about four years later and became eventually parish priest of Blanchardstown.

MR DELANY came to the college in September 1826 and commenced teaching Philosophy in October 1830.[21]

16 Ibid. letter, Crotty to Troy, 18 Aug. 1804. **17** Ibid. **18** Ibid. **19** Ibid. letter, Deane to Troy 14 May 1807. **20** IDA, – E. 22, loose document, 28 July 1804; G. da C., 'St Patrick's school', p. 55. **21** IDA, E. 9.

THE LAST YEARS

JOHN DUNN was rector from the departure of Dr Crotty in 1811 until 1823. A very controversial figure, he was a Dublin diocesan priest, the first student sent to the college by Dr Carpenter after its restoration in 1778. When he had finished his studies, he agreed to stay on to supervise the Philosophy course in 1788. He returned to Ireland in 1791. He was appointed rector in 1811, apparently, with Dr Troy's approval. The records available abound with complaints against him, although Father Daly speaks highly of him. He was in Dublin in 1820 and made arrangements for the running of the parish of Clondalkin, until he returned in 1823 as its parish priest.[22]

MR EGAN came to the college as a pensioner at £20 a year, in May 1827.[23]

JOHN FLYNN left Lisbon to return to his diocese of Elphin in 1791; he had studied at the college, although 'not of the foundation'.[24]

PETER HAMILL was in the college in 1830 on half-pension, and he deposited ten sovereigns with the rector.[25]

HAY, PATRICK O'CONNOR HAY – See O'CONNOR.

DANIEL HORAN, from diocese of Dublin was ordained by Dr Carpenter in 1785. He studied at the college and asked to stay on, at the end of his studies, to 'revise' his course in October 1791. He died in 1794.[26]

JOHN JENNET had been a student in the Irish College, Lille; he came to Lisbon in 1789 and when asked to take the oath, as was customary after six months' residence, decided to leave.[27]

HYACINTH JOYCE, from the archdiocese of Tuam, served as rector from 1823. He had gone to Brazil as chaplain of a Portuguese nobleman in 1807. The appointment of Irish priests to such posts in aristocratic households became quite common at that time. He returned in 1822 and resided at the college. Reputed to be very influential at court, was a friend of Dr C. McNally, bishop of Clonfert, who wrote to him in 1846, sending a banker's order for £60, and thanking him for arranging the delivery of some fine Portuguese wines to Clonfert.[28]

---

22 DDA, letters, Daly to Troy, 22 July 1791; Dunn to Troy, 9 Aug 1822; *Reportorium Novum* 1/2 (1956) 490.   **23** IDA, E. 9.   **24** DDA, letter, Daly to Troy, 6 July 1797.   **25** IDA, E. 9.   **26** DDA, letter, Daly to Troy, 22 July 1791; M.J. Curran, *Reportorium Novum*, 1/2 (1956) 488 & 490.   **27** DDA, letter Daly to Troy 21 July 1790.   **28** Ibid. letter, 1822; IDA, letter, McNally to Joyce, 12 May 1846.

THE IRISH COLLEGE AT LISBON

NICHOLAS KEARNS, also from the diocese of Dublin, was a student at the Irish College, Bordeaux, and was appointed to teach a course in Philosophy in Lisbon in 1785. He seems to have been somewhat unhappy in Lisbon, had health problems, and, according to Father Michael Daly, most of them were in his imagination. He decided early in 1787 that he wished to go back to Ireland and finally left before 13 April 1788. He was a curate in Meath St, Dublin, and was briefly arrested in June 1798. He 'attended Lord Edward Fitzgerald in his last moments.'[29]

THOMAS KELLY, from diocese of Kilalla, was sent, without prior arrangement, to the college by the bishop of Killala, Dr Bellow, who thought, mistakenly, that he was entitled to send a new recruit, whenever one of his had left the college. This was not how the system worked; the system was that each of the four ecclesiastical provinces of Ireland was entitled to send two candidates, whenever a vacancy occurred. The candidates were rotated among all the dioceses of each province. However, the young man was strongly recommended by Crotty and Redmond, both professors in the college, and eventually was allowed to stay. In 1804 Kelly left, because of indisposition.[30]

FATHER LENNON left for Dublin on 14 March 1807.[31]

MICHAEL MC DERMOTT entered the college on 19 May 1825 and deposited six sovereigns with the rector for his maintenance.[32]

JOHN MC EVILY was in the college in December 1830 and deposited four sovereigns.[33]

BRIAN MAC MANUS, a parish priest from the diocese of Elphin, is mentioned by Bishop George Plunket of Elphin, as having studied in the Irish College, Lisbon, in a letter dated 4 October 1823.[34]

Rev. MADDEN came to the college in 1823, said Masses for intentions of Conde de Pena Fiel in 1823, and for the President of the English College in 1824. Dr George Plunket of Elphin in a letter to Dr Dunn said that this student was a nephew of Father MacManus, above, and had been in the

---

29 *Reportorium Novum* 1/2 (1956), 489; DDA, letters Daly to Troy, 20 May 1787; 6 Feb. 1788; D. Keogh, 'The French Disease', (Dublin, 1993), pp 172–3.
30 DDA, letters, Daly to Troy, 18 Apr. 1795; Crotty to Troy, 19 Sept. 1804.
31 DDA, letter J. Joy Deane to Troy, 14 May 1807.   **32** IDA, E. 9.   **33** Ibid.
34 IDA, E. 11, letter Dr G. Plunkett to J. Dunn, 4 Oct. 1823.

Irish College at Paris for eighteen months before returning to Ireland as an invalid. He had been ordained and was now sent to Lisbon 'to prosecute his studies'.[35]

EDWARD MALLEY, from diocese of Clonfert, came to the college in 1831 with a letter from his bishop.[36]

JOHN MANNION is also mentioned in Dr Plunket's letter in 1823: 'Mr Mannion, who affected being delicate some time since, is, I am informed, become a school master in Lisbon. He thinks, I am told, that he will make more money of his school than he would on the mission, and money, it appears, and not the salvation of souls is his object. I am at the present moment much hurried about – the first day I have a leisure hour I shall write to the Patriarch of Lisbon to suspend him.' Mannion (also found as Morrison), signed the letter written to Dr Troy in 1822 regarding the state of the college.[37]

WILLIAM MANNION was sent to Lisbon by Dr Costello, bishop of Clonfert, whose successor, Dr Thomas Coen, wrote in 1797 to the college rector regarding a dimissorial letter for this student, promised by Dr Costello, but because of his defective memory in his later years never sent. It is now sent by him.[38]

THOMAS MULLEN, from the diocese of Dublin, came to the college, in 1797, with a letter from Dr Troy for the rector. He indicated that he wished to become a subject of the house.[39]

JOHN MURPHY, from diocese of Cork, returned there in 1791 having finished his course. He wished to stay on to teach, but his bishop, Dr Moylan, needed him.[40] He was bishop of Cork, 1815–47.

PATRICK MURRAY was a priest of the diocese of Clonfert appointed to succeed Joyce. There is a letter to Dr Joyce from Bishop McNally requesting information about him in 1846.[41]

THOMAS NEVILLE, from diocese of Ferns, was one of the signatories of the letter of 1822.[42]

---

35 Ibid. **36** IDA, E. 16, letter Dr O. Kelly to Dr Joyce, 19 Mar. 1831. **37** IDA, E. 11. **38** IDA, E. 16, letter Thomas Coen to rector, 16 May 1833. **39** DDA, letter Daly to Troy, 12 June 1797. **40** Ibid, letter Daly to Troy, 6 July 1797. **41** IDA, Dr McNally to Joyce, 12 May 1846. **42** DDA 1822.

PATRICK O'CONNOR HAY, of the diocese of Dublin, was professor of Philosophy and Theology in the college and was one of the signatories of the letter of 1822. At the time he was preceptor to the dukes of Cadaval and Lafoës.[43]

PATRICK O'HAGAN was the only professor left in the college in 1804. Crotty says he was a former student of his but a man impossible to live with.[44]

PAUL O'SULLIVAN OP succeeded Fr Russell as rector of St Patrick's College in 1902, which was then in the possession of the Irish Dominicans in Lisbon.[45]

REV MR QUIN, from diocese of Clonfert, was in the college in 1831.[46]

MR REDMOND, a collegian in the college, remained on to commence a course in Philosophy in October 1795. He returned to Ireland in 1804 and Dr Crotty sadly remarked, 'We shall be very lame without him'.[47]

PATRICK B. RUSSELL OP was nominated as rector of St Patrick's on 7 May 1861. The bishops of Ireland, fearing that the Portuguese would seize the college, decided to appoint a member of the Dominican Order in Lisbon as titular rector of St Patrick's at a meeting in the pro-cathedral, Dublin, on 6 December 1859. He was to hold the office and possession of the college on their behalf. He died on 15 November 1901, and Father Paul O'Sullivan OP was appointed to succeed him. During his rectorship, when he was in London in 1886, he had appointed Father Hickey OP to act for him in all matters concerning the Irish College, including rents and the sale of a piece of land belonging to St Patrick's in September 1886.[48]

WILLIAM SHERRY was ordained in Lisbon in 1816 and was a student of St Patrick's. In 1822 he wrote a long letter to Dr Troy thanking him for the recommendation that he should succeed Dr John Dunn. He informed Dr Troy that there was no possibility of Dr Dunn giving over the rectorship, and complained bitterly about the treatment he received from Dunn.[49]

---

43 Ibid. 44 DDA, letter Daly to Troy, 3 Apr. 1795 and Crotty to Troy, 18 Aug. 1804. 45 IDA, E. 28 & 46. 46 IDA, E.16, Dr. O. Kelly to Dr Joyce, letter 19 Mar. 1831. 47 DDA, letter Daly to Troy, 3 Apr. 1795 and Crotty to Troy, 7 May 1803. 48 IDA, E. 28, 29, 46. 49 DDA, letter, Sherry to Troy, 27 July 1822.

THE LAST YEARS

JOÃO ANTÓNIO VIANNA, of Bahia, a Brazilian student of the college, completed his course satisfactorily – '*alumno interno neste Real Colegio*, an intern student, attended classes in Rhetoric, Philosophy and Geometry. His certificate was signed by Hyacinth Joyce on 31 May 1825.[50]

THE FINAL STATE OF THE COLLEGE

Three former students, living in Lisbon, wrote a letter in 1822 to Dr Troy which gives a very disturbing picture of the college and its lamentable state at that time, twelve years before it finally closed. The letter is signed by Fathers Patrick O'Connor Hay, of the archdiocese of Dublin, formerly of the college and at that time preceptor to the dukes of Cadaval and Lafoens, John Mannion (Morrison is also given), of the diocese of Elphin, then preceptor to the viscount of Maniquo, and Thomas Neville, of the diocese of Ferns, who was resident in St Patrick's College, Lisbon. The letter is very lengthy, closely written on five sides of three pages of foolscap paper. This extraordinary letter begins:

> We the undersigned secular priests from different Dioceses of Ireland, influenced neither by prejudice, malice, hatred or envy, but actuated by pure zeal for our Religion, the honor of our country, and our individual and conjoined duty, stimulated moreover by the ignominious disgrace of the long and notorious misgovernment of our National College at Lisbon, have come to the tardy resolution of laying before your Grace as exact a statement as we can collect, of the different vicissitudes this house has undergone, the periods of its prosperity, deterioration, and nearly final degradation, together with a synopsis of the means which we think may be most conducive to its restoration and consequently to the honor and utility of the Irish Mission.

They trace the history of the college up to the suppression of the Jesuits and the sequestration of the college and its property, until Father Daly, with the support of Dr Troy, re-established Ireland's claims to the house. They point out that Mr Crotty on his succession to Mr Daly found 'a well stored college coffer which Mr Daly had amassed for the purpose of either

50 IDA, E. 12.

repairing the college or building a new one; neither being done, how the immense sum has disappeared is known only to Mr Crotty alone'. Based on the facts, it does not appear possible that Crotty could have inherited a 'well-stored coffer' since he had complained to Dr Troy that the royal grants were several years in arrears.[51]

However, they further state that under his government things were in a reasonable state for about four or five years. They point out that Mr Crotty wrote to Dr Troy for a successor and got 'one that has proved himself highly qualified to continue the destroying system nearly down to annihilation'. This was the Rev. Mr Dunn who ruled the college for twelve years. During his administration they claim they can find 'but three students, one of whom paid full pension, the second was only partly free and the third, was a secular, sent by no authority and not acknowledged by any Bishop, either before or after his return to Ireland.'

They continue:

> 'Here Yr Grace may naturally ask, as numberless others both native and foreigners, have done from time to time, why are there no students in St Patrick's College? What is done with the rents of this house? Why is the college not repaired? To these questions we find ourselves incapable to give a possible answer ...' However, they say bluntly that 'if we do not infer, that the present Rector is guilty of sacriligeous peculation, we must infer, that he is guilty of deception towards Portugal; fraudalence towards his own country and of callous insensibility to each and every interest of this poor, degraded house'.

Their description of the house is shocking:

> It sits sadly eminent as the doleful monument of national delinquency and disgrace; its situation beautiful; itself all deformity; its circumjacent buildings in the highest state of Architectural elegance; the college as gloomy ruins; its exterior frightful; its interior loathsome and filthy; its timbers are in the last stage of putrefaction; its doors, floors, and partitions shattered and squalid; its chinks and crevices are crowded with nasty and venemous reptiles, and it is all covered over with nauseous and noxious vermin. The Church we shall not mention, it admits of no description. Whoever sees it now and

---

51 DDA, letter, three signatures, to Troy 1822.

remembers its former days may with every justice exclaim, 'Haec antigua Domus'. Such is the melancholy, yet rather flattering picture we are forced to exhibit to Your Grace of the Doleful mismanagement of this once respected College.

Certainly, it appears that a bad situation existed in the college for some time before and after Father Daly's death. He had wanted to retire from the rectorship prior to 1795. His letters to Dr Troy during the years 1780–95, when Troy was bishop of Ossory and later archbishop of Dublin, attest to this. His early efforts, for over twenty years, from 1758 to 1779, were devoted to getting back the college property and income. After that time there were concerns with the constant wars, lawsuits, teaching-staff problems, and even the difficulties of getting students from the various Irish dioceses.

Not content with the astonishing letter to Dr Troy, the trio of concerned priests drafted a letter to the hapless Rector Dunn himself. In it there is an ultimatum. This letter may never have been sent to Dunn. Obviously, a copy of it was sent to the archbishop of Dublin and this is still preserved in the Diocesan Archives. The letter they proposed to send to Dunn is strong stuff. Unfortunately, the wily rector was well ahead of them. He sent an immediate letter to Dr Troy nominating Dr Hyacinth Joyce as successor and indicating that, as soon as he had been broken in to the job, he himself would leave for his parish in Dublin.

It is the opinion of the three writers of the letter that the rector 'rules over an empty house and that in ruins'; that the college during his regime has never answered the laudable ends for which it was meant and never will under his direction. They beg him to resign and insist that they address him as a fellow-priest. If he does not heed their advice, they give him notice that he shall be called upon by proper authority to answer for every particular of his administration. They accuse him of pretence of resigning over more than six years in an effort to ward off the long-impending storm caused by his mismanagement. 'Had all this crying degradation been occasioned either by ravages of war or the tyranny or iniquity of the Government, they would 'wait and pray for a favourable change'; but they 'cannot blame these hypothetical outside causes.' To them it is clear that 'infidelity, self-interest and indolence' have been the cause of the desolation of the college. In support of this view they cite the opposite situation in the English College, due to 'their unremitting diligence, their assiduity , industry and love of their religion and country'. In the Irish College a school was also set-up for the education of youth but was instituted under different principles from that of the English College. The emoluments received from the project in the Irish College were divided between the rector and his two associates, whereas the English had opened their school with the laudable object of applying the profits thereof to the augmentation of their ecclesiastical seminary. Their church is elegant and their house is the most superb edifice in its vicinity. The writers of the letter conclude that the rector must be dismissed if any reform is to take place.

However, the rector was too clever for the three rather disingenuous clerics. The postscript to their letter tells it all:

> Here Yr Grace may be astonished at the paucity of signatures, we are so, too, and this is partly the cause of the present adjoinder. We expected to have more names to support this remonstrance [but] when it was presented to a certain individual [named Hynes, who had hitherto been clamourously importunate for the attainment of this object] he refused to sign it for the sinister purpose of having his cousin appointed to the rectorship, which Mr Dunn had previously offered him, as he had done to almost every Irish priest in Lisbon, without the most distant intention of verifying any of these unsolicited fictitious pre-offers. This recusant, ... considering the title of informer to be more his interest than that of regenerator, disclosed the whole business to Mr Dunn, who with terrified activity hastened off to the King, and proposed the Rev. John [*sic*] Joyce as his successor to the Rectorship of St Patrick's College. By this act he effected a division between us, and thought to upset our plan, and by this act he also gains time for further machinations, knowing that the King's Council will determine nothing without mature deliberation and will finally decide the business by a *concursus*, to which Mr Joyce is totally inadequate – But should it, through any fatality be concluded, ... the prospect is both sickening and appalling ...

It is difficult to make a judgment on this remarkable letter. Certainly, there is other evidence to support the estimate of the Rev. John Dunn as difficult, intriguing, perhaps two-faced, and somewhat Machiavellian in his dealings with his fellow-clerics. In view of the bishop of Clonfert's letter mentioned earlier and his obvious disapproval of Mannion becoming a 'schoolmaster' instead of a minister of religion, for which he was trained and educated over many years, the whole matter becomes very convoluted.

THE LAST YEARS

The college limped on for a further twelve years under the government of Dr Joyce and lastly, under Patrick Murray. In its last years the Irish College, Lisbon, was only a shadow of its former self. When it finally closed its doors to students in 1834; it was administered by the Irish Dominicans, of Corpo Santo, until its eventual disposal in the early twentieth century. Father Patrick Russell, the Irish Dominican who was given the care of the college after the closure, was happy to report to the bishop of Kilmore, Dr Leahy, that since 1861 the house and the church which he had managed to repair, even including a new roof, was being put to good use by a zealous Franciscan priest. This man, Father Beirão, and some ladies of the Third Order of St Francis, use the house for a free school to teach the poor female children of the neighbourhood. Father Beirão offers Mass in the chapel, teaches cathechism and hears confessions daily. Father Russell tells the bishop, that the area around the Irish College was 'much in need of a priest's care'.[52]

The college, as we have seen from the lists of students who were ordained and returned to the Irish Mission, turned out a respectable number of priests over the period from 1590 to the last years of the eighteenth century. When conditions deteriorated at the beginning of the nineteenth century, both financially and politically, it was felt that the college should be sold. But it was not until 1859, after the college came into the possession of the Irish Dominicans in Lisbon and was maintained by them, that plans were afoot to sell the Lisbon College. Some of the Irish bishops met in Dublin in the pro-cathedral in December of that year to discuss the question. Those prelates who were not able to attend were circulated for their opinions. In his letter of reply, Dr James Brown, bishop of Kilmore, voiced the sentiments of many at the time: 'I ... very much regret to see those old and important establishments in ruins or lost to this country.'[53] The college was not, in fact, sold at that time but it passed out of Irish ownership at the beginning of the twentieth century and it is certainly true to say that the sentiments of the wise bishop of yesteryear would find agreement even in the Ireland of today.

---

[52] IDA, E. 23, draft letter Russell to Dr Leahy of Kilmore, undated.   [53] IDA, E. 24, letter James Browne of Kilmore to Russell, 15 Dec. 1859.

CHAPTER 8

Conclusion

One might well ask why Lisbon was chosen as the place to set up an Irish seminary in the 1590s. The likely reason was, presumably, accessibility. The origins of the traffic that passed between the island of Ireland and the Iberian peninsula are lost in the mists of time. There were travellers from Ireland who found their way, at an early stage, to the shrine of St James at Santiago de Compostela, one of the earliest Christian shrines in Europe. Like most of the other Northern Europeans the Irish also made their way to the Crusades via the Portuguese ports. The Portuguese were a race of mariners, navigators and explorers.[1] It is known that the Irish coast was familiar to Portuguese seafarers. A glance at the map indicates that the Portuguese Atlantic ports and the Irish maritime cities, such as Waterford, Cork, Galway Limerick and even smaller fishing villages, such as Ardmore as mentioned already, were on the old trade routes. In addition to the ease of access, there was in Portugal at that time, in common with most of the other Catholic kingdoms in the late sixteeenth century, a wave of sympathy, for their persecuted fellow-Catholics fleeing from religious persecution and, indeed, from foreign domination. It is also probable that the Portuguese felt an affinity with the Irish because they were themselves then under domination by their nearest neighbour, Spain, and had earlier suffered from long, Moorish occupation.

When the Irish college was founded in Lisbon, Spain was very much in favour of helping the Irish against the English. Later, however, their ignominious defeat at Kinsale, would lead to a policy of appeasement towards England. The founding of Irish Colleges in Spanish territory was the Spanish way of helping to maintain their role as the strong leader of the Counter-Reformation in Ireland by having aspirants to the priesthood trained, in Spanish-controlled seminaries, to combat the influence of the Protestant Reformation in Ireland. The financial help received by the Irish College, Lisbon may have originally come from a Spanish monarch but

1 One thinks immediately of Henry the Navigator, Vasco da Gama and Fernão de Magalhães (Magellan).

undeniably the same generosity was shown when the house of Braganza ascended the throne in 1640. In spite of the many treaties and agreements between Britain and Portugal, and the 'favoured nation' status accorded to the British over the centuries, the Portuguese felt a genuine sympathy for their harshly-treated co-religionists in Ireland.

The Irish collegians were not always the easiest guests within Portugal. They could be troublesome, demanding and were often aggressive in their behaviour. Now and then they champed at the bit of Portuguese authority and were impatient with the ways of their hosts. In general, however, there was a good relationship at local level. As the political conditions and national interests of Portugal changed over the centuries the Irish may have become a thorn-in-the-flesh of the government. It is possible that, if the college had not closed in 1834, the Irish students might have out-stayed their initial welcome, and the Portuguese might have been glad to rid themselves of the 'turbulent priests'.

Even in 1791 the Portuguese First Minister of State had expressed the opinion that perhaps it might be a good idea to set-up seminaries in Ireland.[2] Things were changing in Ireland and, by 1795, Maynooth had been founded and financed by the British, who doubtless, had realized that there was no hope of stemming the flow of priests coming back to Ireland from the continent. They were naturally worried, for example, about how much those priests trained in France might have been influenced by the revolutionary spirit after 1789, and what influence they might have on the populace of Ireland, or even of their own island. It must be said that with the founding of St Patrick's College, in Maynooth, it was becoming increasingly difficult to get suitable 'subjects' for the Lisbon college. The setting-up of this college in Ireland effectively sounded the death-knell of the Lisbon College, which was already slowly declining from an incurable malady. There was now, in effect, a rivalry between Maynooth and the continental colleges. Most of the Irish colleges in France faced ruin and closure at the time of the French Revolution and, in many cases, their students were sent to Spain or Portugal. Students from the English colleges were also transferred to the English colleges in Lisbon or Valladolid. The suppression of the religious orders in many countries, in particular, the Jesuits in Portugal 1759 and in Spain in 1769, was another nail in the coffin of the continental seminaries. The Peninsular War had,

2 DDA, letter, Daly to Troy, 22 July 1791.

as we saw, an adverse effect on the Lisbon college and, after the Napoleonic wars, there was what we might call a recession.

Catholic Emancipation came finally in 1829 but, even so, pre-Famine Ireland must have been a grim place. Things were very bad economically and there were many local famines in the years before, what we call now, the Great Famine of 1847. While this was true of the whole country, the West of Ireland, mainly the counties of Connacht, was in a deplorable state. The rector, Hyacinth Joyce, who went to Brazil with the royal party and was reputed to be very influential at court in post-war Lisbon, came from one of the worst-hit areas of the country. A letter from the bishop of Clonfert, Dr Oliver Kelly, who visited Westport in 1831 in order to try and get some relief for the starving people, makes very harrowing reading. This was several years before the Great Famine:

> I have come to this part of the country a few days ago to endeavour, as far as in my powers, to procure relief for the famishing peasantry of this country. You will have read in the papers a melancholy account of the prevailing misery and distress owing to the failure of the potato crops and other causes, I have only to assure you that these accounts are not exaggerated, and that any picture which may be drawn of the actual misery and privation of the poor in this country cannot be overcharged.[3]

A letter to Rector Joyce, from his brother, Patrick, written from Fahy, Westport, County Mayo in 1830, gives a very sorry account of life for a tenant-farmer in Mayo in the 1830s. Patrick Joyce tells his brother about conditions near Westport a year before Bishop Kelly's visit:

> We were made very happy lately by a Schoolmaster of the name of Donnelly coming to reside in the Parish ... but there is so little encouragement for him in this place that he is talking of going away, which will put us to the expense of sending our little John to Castlebar or some other place for his instruction which we are very barely able to do, rents being so high, and the times are worse in this county than were ever remembered. [There is] no money in circulation and the long family I have to support leaves me in great

---

3 IDA, letter Dr O. Kelly to Dr J. Joyce, 14 (or 19) Mar. 1831.

hardship, though I struggle very hard for them. This season, in consequence of sending John to school, and my own health not being strong, I was obliged to hire a boy to assist me in my Spring work. I would struggle to the last rather than to take John from school and for this, my dear brother, I rely upon your promise to assist me ... This is the third letter I have written to you since I heard from you [*in 1828*], and having never got any answer, I have been very uneasy lest you might have been displeased with me ... therefore, I entreat of you to let me have a few lines which might relieve my mind. I hope, my dear brother, that you will not think that we ran through or made any bad use of the generous remittance you sent us in 1828. We paid £7 for a cow, and £9 for a horse, both of which we still have, and with the horse I am enabled sometimes to earn a trifle, but lately no work or employment of any kind is going forward.

The whole family are in good health as formerly – no change of any kind has taken place amongst them lately – I have a son by Biddy named Andy – a strong boy, who has a great wish to go out to you.

There is little news to write you. The great Catholic question is now happily past, and Ireland never was so tranquil as it is at this time only the distress is great. Many are emigrating to America this year and more preparing to do so the next. For unless there is some change the poor cannot stand it. We hear that it is much the same in England. Since the war trade has declined – the linen trade, which you may remember, so flourishing amongst us is gone – a hank of yarn 3*d* and brown linen 4 ½*d* and 5*d* per yard. The Spring, which gave us great hopes about a fortnight ago of having a fine season, has suddenly changed. We have had the last week constant rain and cold weather so that our Spring sowing is very backward. In hopes that this will reach you safely and in good health and that you will be pleased to acknowledge this letter which would be the greatest pleasure you could bestow on your very obed. and humble brother.

Patt Joyce.

Bridget's son is going to the same school as our son, John – but there is little chance that the school will continue the times are so bad that few are able to keep their children at it.'[4]

---

[4] Ibid., letter, Patrick Joyce to Dr J. Joyce, 23 Apr. 1830.

Clearly this letter is a desperate cry for help from a man almost overcome by his poverty and misfortune and his anxiety for his children and their education. It appears that the families of many of the rectors, and indeed, of the students suffered a great deal of hardship in the very bad times at home in Ireland. Often families had to make great sacrifices so that their children could study for the priesthood abroad. Father Daly, in his letters to Dr Troy, on occasions mentions that he was badly needed back home, and Dr Crotty informed the archbishop that his conscience troubled him through his neglect of his aged mother; he was an only child, and could do little for her support. The poverty of their lives and their dedication to the welfare of their students are often overlooked. Indeed, the financial status of the students' families was also a matter of grave concern to the students themselves during their studies.

There is no doubt that all the Irish colleges had financial problems. Life in the colleges was spartan; in general, rectors and teachers were unpaid, usually receiving only their board and lodging. While the Jesuits were running the colleges this was not a major problem as they had the support of their Order. When the secular priests took over, after the suppression of the Society of Jesus things were somewhat different. They had virtually no financial support from their dioceses. This was possibly the reason why it was so difficult to keep teachers on the staff in the later years of the Lisbon college. It was inevitable, when the opportunity presented itself – to earn money as a teacher outside the college or as a preceptor in a nobleman's household – that some of the priests found it difficult to refuse.

LIVING CONDITIONS

Nicholas Kearns, teacher in the college for three years, decided in 1787 to return to Ireland both because of his health and 'the disagreeable state of the college'. Father Daly believed, as other did, that his chief disorder 'is in the imagination' and that Kearns suffered from a nervous complaint. A letter from Daly to Dr Troy[5] about this matter gives us one of the few glimpses of the living conditions in the college at that time. The rector dismisses Kearns criticisms of the state of the college, saying that before he came to Lisbon he was told formally what to expect – that the 'house was a ruin and it requires a degree of courage to inhabit'. He also occupied the

5 DDA, letters, Daly to Troy, 1 Sept. 1787 & 6 Feb. 1788.

apartment that the Jesuit rectors occupied in succession, with this difference 'that they had no separate room for this bed, and he has'. He cannot conceive how an apartment 'that satisfied a dignified Regious [sic] man, may not content a secular priest'.

'As to table', he continues, 'it is such as is sufficient, but certainly not such as can be envied; but even such as it is, it is expensive, for this is the dearest capital in Europe for all the necessities of life'. Kearns was permitted to keep all his mass offerings, he was fed frugally, he owns, but 'he has a breakfast of chocolate, at dinner sixteen ounces of boiled beef or mutton, with soup and vegetables, some cheese or fruit, according to the season and wine; at supper eight ounces of meat, the rest at dinner'. It is to be assumed that the collegians received the same fare.

As regards dress, he admits there has been some bickering between himself and Kearns:

> There are two other houses of the same nature with ours, but much better funded; the Irish Dominicans, whose superior and Masters clothe themselves and pay for their own washing; and for this are allowed by the house but two masses a week; all the rest are for the community. The other is an English mission house for secular priests; where the superior and masters are each clad at a very moderate expense, which Mr Kearns found upon enquiry, but thinks their custom not worthy of imitation. As the finances of this house are yet so low, I take nothing from it, not even washing, except what I eat, which is not an atom different from what it described above, and even breakfast I provide at my own expense.

I found only one other reference to food – some ledger entries for supplies of food, around the early nineteenth century; bacon, bacon fat, potatoes, rice, firkins of butter, kegs of tripe, beef, mixed tea, Dutch white beans and dried cod.[6]

Students were told to bring a lot of baggage. As well as many articles of strong clothing, they were expected to bring a mattress, sheets, blankets as well as books, chiefly in Latin and Greek (with for good measure a Greek lexicon and works by Homer) and any other school books which they might have. The student, it goes without saying, was to be of high moral calibre and genteel education.[7]

6 IDA, E. 22.   7 Ibid., letter, Daly to Troy, 7 May 1803.

In the early years of the Lisbon college there was a strong enrolment of students from the southern half of the island of Ireland. The predominant dioceses were Waterford/Lismore, Cashel, Ossory, Ferns; Limerick, Cork, Cloyne, Kilmore, Killaloe also show some collegians; Tuam, Galway and Clonfert come next. Meath and Dublin have a good showing in later years. Since numbers were much reduced after the re-opening of the college in the late eighteenth century, there was an attempt to choose two students from each archdiocese in turn, with the choice based on a sequence of the dioceses within each archdiocese.

In the beginning many of the students came from the wealthy classes in, for example, Waterford, Cork, Meath or Dublin, but as conditions in Ireland worsened during the seventeenth and eighteenth centuries, so, too, did the financial status of the collegians in St Patrick's. Future research may help us to establish the social pool from which students for the priesthood were drawn and also how many chose to remain in Portugal rather than return to Ireland. The *Register of popish clergy* of 1704 indicates that only thirty-two of those registered as parish priests, were ordained in Portugal, and their parishes were in the counties of Cavan, Cork, Dublin, Galway, Kilkenny, Louth, Meath, Tipperary, Waterford Westmeath, Wexford. This almost exactly reflects the enrolment stated above.

The Irish College at Lisbon, like all of the Irish continental colleges, was important in its early years as a contact centre for the Irish there, and functioned as a social and political centre for the expatriate community. It assumed a certain importance as an unofficial 'consulate' for the Irish, travelling to and from Lisbon; as it was for the Irish who settled down and became integrated. The first of these categories included the clerics who studied there and returned to the mission in Ireland;[8] important historical figures, such as James Fitzmaurice Fitzgerald, who in the years 1577–9 operated periodically out of Lisbon in an attempt to raise a military expedition to Ireland; doctors who practised among the English-speaking community, and invalids who came to Lisbon for their health because of its mild, curative air;[9] military men, whether belonging to the Irish

---

[8] Apart from the secular priests from St Patrick's there were many who belonged to the various relegous orders in Portugal-Jesuits, Dominicans, Franciscans and others who are outside the scope of this study.   [9] One interesting case was a delicate young woman, sent out to Lisbon by her guardian in 1792, thought to be consumptive, or having 'the king's disease', a swelling of the glands all over the body, especially the neck and thought curable only by the touch of a king. She

CONCLUSION

brigades on the continent, or with the British armies which became a feature of life in Lisbon after the Napoleonic Wars. I have already mentioned the duke of Wellington and General William Carr Beresford, two well-known figures born in Ireland who figured in the Napoleonic War in Portugal, the former the greatly admired hero of the Peninsular War, the latter reputed to have been the most hated man in Lisbon, '*este Britânico odioso*'.[10] Other distinguished figures with Irish connections were Percy Clinton Sydney Smythe, sixth Viscount Strangford, graduate of Trinity College, Dublin and friend of Tom Moore, the Irish composer; Lord Robert Fitzgerald, Lord Londonderry and Lord Tyrawley, all British diplomats with Irish-sounding names.

Included in the second category are those who settled in Lisbon and became integrated, some of whom were described by the British envoy, Castres, as the 'obscure Irish of the poorer sort'. These Irish lived and worked in Lisbon about the time of the earthquake; one of the settled Irish immigrants who receives mention in Rose Macauley's work on Portugal includes an old Irish widow, Mrs Williams, who kept a famous hotel in Lisbon, 'upon the point of a lofty hill called Buenos Ayres'; the house afterwards achieved fame as the British embassy.[11]

THE O'NEILLS OF PORTUGAL

I am pleased to end this work on the history of the Irish College of St Patrick in Lisbon with the story of one of Ireland's great families, the O'Neills of Clanaboy, who as the O'Neills of Portugal added so much lustre not only to their country of origin but also to their adopted land.[12]

The O'Neills of Portugal descend from Shane O'Neill, born in Kilmore, County Cavan, son of Conn O'Neill and Cecilia O'Hanlon. He came to Portugal in the 1740s with two of his brothers.[13] He brought with him

---

made a good recovery and returned home in 1793. Dr Troy had charged Michael Daly with her protection and requested him to advance her money as she needed it, to be repaid by her guardian. **10** Macauley, *They went to Portugal too* (Manchester, 1990), pp 198–231. **11** Macauley, *They went to Portugal*, p. 254. **12** This interesting account of the history of the O'Neills of Portugal is entirely based on an account of the family given to me by Dom Hugo O'Neill, and compiled by himself in consultation with his nephew, Pedro Teixeiro O'Neill, an architect, who is the family historian.' **13** Ibid: 'as he could no longer lead in Ireland the life of a gentleman and all hopes of fighting for the revival of Gaelic rule were lost'.

from Ireland a parchment pedigree in Latin tracing his lineage from Brian Ballach, chief of Clanaboy. He was well-received by the Irish community in Lisbon, particularly by Father Brian Brulaughan, later Frei Bernardo de Santa Rosa, rector of Corpo Santo, who became a close friend and later introduced him to his future wife, Valentina Ferreira Palyart. He died in 1788 and in his lifetime three generations of O'Neills married into other expatriate Irish families, Braughall, Long, Lynch, FitzGibbon and Caffrey.

The next chief of the family was Charles O'Neill (1760–1835) who was educated at St Omer, the English Catholic school in Douai, Normandy, where Daniel O'Connel was a pupil in 1790. Charles married a German heiress and became a partner in her father's merchant house, Torlade & Co., established in Hamburg in 1719 and which later transferred to Setúbal. He developed the company which became the leading exporter of salt and oranges to Scandinavia and the Baltic States. He lived in Setúbal in a beautiful house, Quinta das Machadas, where the present head of the family still lives. He was consul of the United States of America, France and Denmark in Setúbal, was a friend to Pombal, to Queen Maria I, and to her eldest son and heir, José, prince of Brazil, who was godfather to his eldest son, José Maria O'Neill. José Maria took over the leadership of the family, promoted Lisbon Gas Light network, and launched a banking house.

His son, Jorge, married his cousin, Carolina O'Neill, was a keen sportman and traveller, and later took over the company and made it a multinational organization with headquarters in Paris. He was recognized as The O'Neill by the Ulster King at Arms, had a passion for Irish history, acquired a precious collection of Irish history books and was a patron of the Irish cause. He was a friend of Sir Roger Casement, who had been briefly British consul in Lisbon. He built two fine palaces in Cascais and Estoril, which are now museums. He was invited as The O'Neill to the celebrations of Irish Independence in 1925 but died that year. He was a man of brilliant mind.

His son and heir, Hugo, entered the Portuguese Royal Navy, married a great lady and lived bravely through difficult times – the murder of his brother, the assassination of the king and the crown prince, the end of the monarchy and the liquidation of the family business, Torlade & Co, as a result of the financial crash and depression of 1929–30. His elder son, Jorge, succeeded in rebuilding the family fortunes and was, as well, a talented writer and philosopher.

His son, the present holder of the family title, The O'Neill, Hugo O'Neill, has a deep love of Ireland and a keen and extensive knowledge of

CONCLUSION

its history and heritage, and takes enormous pride in the ancient and illustrious family from which he stems; and he cares very much to keep alive his ancient heritage and name.

Through the Irish College, Ireland had a strong, though largely forgotten, relationship with Portugal for several hundred years. Even Rector Crotty had complained in 1804, that the Irish bishops were more interested 'in the spiritual life of Christians in America or Botany Bay' than in the college in Lisbon. In truth, the Irish Church began to look beyond our erstwhile, friends, the Catholic countries of Europe, to the United States of America, Canada, Australia, even Latin America. When Latin declined and English began to dominate this change was copperfastened.

The Irish were lucky to have had friends in their time of need. National memories are short and eaten bread is soon forgotten and we turned away from our continental friends when times got better and our multitudes of refugees sought a new life in the new world. It is essential, nevertheless, to keep alive the memory of our longstanding ties with the Low Countries, France, Spain, Portugal, Italy, Germany, Switzerland and Eastern Euope – our important European heritage, as well as the new links forged over the past two and a half centuries elsewhere.

Bibliography

Borrow, George, *The Bible in Spain* (London, 1842).
Boxer, C.R., *The Portuguese seaborne empire, 1415–1825* (Manchester, reprint 1997).
Brady, W.M., *Episcopal succession*, 3 vols (Rome, 1876).
Cogan, A., *Ecclesiastical history of the diocese of Meath* 3 vols (Dublin, 1870).
Costa, Manuel Gonçalves da, *Fontes inéditas portuguesas para a história de Irlanda* (Braga, 1981).
'Saint Patrick's school of Lisbon', *BHS of Portugal*, 1989, pp 37–57.
Curran, Olive (ed.), *History of the diocese of Meath 1704–1993* (Mullingar, 1995).
Fenning OP, Hugh, 'Irishmen ordained at Lisbon, 1587–1850' *Collectanea Hibernica* (1989–96).
Finegan SJ, Francis (Unpublished), *Biographical dictionary of Irish Jesuits in the time of the Society's third Irish mission, 1598–1773*.
Hogan SJ, Edmund, *Distinguished Irishmen of the sixteenth century* (London, 1894).
Kelly, James and Dáire Keogh (eds), *History of the Catholic diocese of Dublin* (Dublin, 2000).
Keogh, Dáire, *'The French disease': the Catholic church and radicalism in Ireland* (Dublin, 1993).
Lodge, Sir Richard (ed.), *The private correspondence of Sir Benjamin Keane* (London, 1933).
Macauley, Rose, *They went to Portugal* (London, 1946).
—— , *They went to Portugal, too* (Manchester, 1990).
Murphy, D., *Our martyrs* (Dublin, 1896).
Neligan, Agnes (ed.), *The Maynooth Library treasures* (Dublin, 1995).
O'Boyle, James, *The Irish colleges on the continent: their origin and history* (Belfast, 1935).
O'Connor, Thomas (ed.), *The Irish in Europe, 1480–1815* (Dublin, 2001).
Reneghan, L.F., *Collections on Irish church history* (Dublin, 1874).
Richardson, Regina Whelan (ed.), *Salamanca letters* (Maynooth, 1995).
Saraiva, José Hermano, *Portugal: a companion history* (Manchester, 1997).

Shaw, L.M.E., *The Anglo-Portuguese alliance and the English merchants in Portugal, 1654–1810* (Aldershot, 1998).
Silke, John, *Kinsale: the Spanish intervention in Ireland at the end of the Elizabethian wars* (Liverpool, 1970; reprint Dublin, 2000).
Swords, Liam, *Soldiers, scholars, priests* (Paris, 1985).
Walsh, Micheline Kerney, *The Spanish knights of Irish origin*, 4 vols (Dublin, 1960–78).
Walsh, T.J., *The Irish continental college movement* (Dublin, 1973).

Index

Details of rectors of St Patrick's College are given on pages 38–42; names and biographical details of students of the college and relevant dioceses, where known, will be found on pages 55–99 and 118–125. The student names are not included in this index except when they occur elsewhere in the text.

Achonry, diocese of 52, 72
Aguiar, Damião 28
Ajuda palace 41
Alacoque, Margaret Mary 109
Albert, cardinal archduke 25
Alcalá de Henares: see Irish colleges
Almeida, Miguel de 89
Almareleja 90
Annaghduff 93
Antonio, prior of Crato 23n
Archer, Francis 105
Archer, Pierce 55
Ardagh, diocese of 72, 93
Ardee 70
Ardfert, diocese of 65
Armagh, diocese of 33, 45n, 52, 53, 83
Ardmore 18
Ardpatrick 80
Arthurstown 69
Atalaia, condesa de: see Brito, de
Augustinians 14, 76, 84, 91, 92
Azores 43, 44n, 71, 73, 79

Ballentullagh 68
Ballinderry 84
Balmadum 96
Ballyfarmaul 72
Ballynegora 93
Bandini, cardinal 62
Barr, Bartholomew 53
Batalha 27
Bath, Robert 44, 44n
Beauparc 88
Beckford, William 115
Belém 41
Bellow, Dr 122
Bermingham, Francis 18, 116
Bermingham, William 105
Beresford, William 117, 137

Bethal, Robert 103n
Bilbao 18, 116
Biblioteca Nacional 7
Biondi, Fabio 27
Blanchardstown 120
boarders 56n, 110
Bologna 16n
Bom Sucesso 23, 23n
Borrow, George 115
Bowman: see Archer
Braga 54n
Braganza, Catarina, duchess of 23n,
Braganza, Catherine of, queen 64
Brandini, Aldo 27
Braughall family 138
Brazil 43, 78, 81, 117, 118, 121
Brito, D. Iria de 23n
Brown, Eustace 51
Brown, James 129
Brulaughan, Brian, Frei Bernardo de Santa
    Rosa OP 138
Burghley, William Cecil, Lord 33
Burgo, John de 51
Butler, Alban 68, 75, 82
Byrne, Edmund 92
Byron, Lord 115

Cadaval, duke of 89, 124
Caffrey family 138
Caldeyra, Francisco 110
Cantwell, Michael 86
Capuchins, 14
Carbery, Nicholas 112
Carew, Richard 43
Carey, Patrick 113
Cahir 84
Carmelites 14
Carpenter, John 50, 51, 71, 77, 103, 121
Carthy, Denis 112

[143]

Carton 96
Carvalho da Costa 106
Carvalho e Melo, Sebastião José: see Pombal
Cascais 138
Casement, Sir Roger 138
Cashel 42, 45n, 51, 52, 53, 60, 62, 64, 71, 72, 76, 79, 84, 98
Cashel cathedral 95
Castelo Branco, Duarte de 27
Castlekelly 65
Castlepollard 66
Castletown 83
Castres, Abraham 100, 101, 137
Castro, Miguel de 52
Catholic education 13, 14, 47–9
Catholic emancipation 13, 42
Catholic kingdoms 14
Charles II 96
Charneca 107
Chaves, Paolo de 3
Christ Church 95
Clara 71
Clare, Edward 55
Clement III 109n
Clondalkin 71
Clonfert 40, 44n, 51, 52, 72, 83, 121, 123
Clogher 75
Cloniske 66
Clonleigh 92
Clonmel 48, 59, 94, 99
Clontarf 82
Cloyne: see Cork
Coen, Thomas 123
Coimbra 42, 44, 54n, 65, 74, 84, 93; university of 39n, 41, 43, 44, 46, 50, 53, 60, 61, 65, 66, 71, 85, 86, 96, 98, 99
Comerford, Patrick 51
Colegio da Purifição: see Évora, university of
College of the Nobles (Colégio dos Nobres) 104, 105
confiscation of St Patricks 40, 40n, 125
Connor, Bernard 55
convictores: see boarders
Cork, Cloyne, Ross, dioceses, 41, 51, 53, 61, 66, 73, 78, 85, 87, 94, 97, 105, 118, 123, 124, 125–6, 134
Corkran, John 112
Corish, Patrick 20
Cornelio de S Patricio: see O'Mahony
Corpo Santo 22, 22n, 29, 34, 52, 106, 138
Costa, Bras (Baltasar) da 28
Costa, M. Gonçalves da 20

Costello, Dr 123
Counter-Reformation 14, 23, 130
Couto, Diego SJ 34
Cridan: see Riordan
Cristianos novos 32, 32n
Crotty, Bartholomew 41, 53, 78, 105, 118, 122, 123, 124, 125–6, 134, 139
da Cruz, Guilielmo 44
Cunha, Nuno da 40
Cusack, James 112
Curtis, Patrick 114
Cuzco, bishop of 32

Daly, Michael 41, 46, 102–5, 117, 121, 125, 127, 134
David, Richard: see Richard Daniel
Deane, Joseph Joy 105
Delgado, Joao SJ 38
Derry 66, 91
Dillon, Peter 110
Doliscoren 76
Dominicans Irish 14, 21, 81, 90, 90n, 124, 129
Donabate 78
Donnelly, Joseph OFM 55
Dowdall, Patrick 109
Down and Connor diocese 83
Drogheda 72, 85, 97
Dromlane 83
Duarte (Edward) prince 27
Dubin, Nicholas 87
Dublin 18, 18a, 19, 23, 50, 51, 59, 60, 62, 63, 64, 66, 68, 70, 71, 72, 73, 77, 78, 79, 87, 89, 90, 92, 93, 94, 96, 103, 118, 119, 122, 124
Dublin Castle 96
Dugin, John Baptist 34, 38, 39n, 42
Duleek 85
Dum exquisita, papal bull 14
Duncormack 87
Dundalk 75, 83
Dunn, John 41, 105, 122, 124, 126, 127, 128
Dunsany 95
Dunshaughlin 93, 99

earthquake 35, 40, 67, 100–104
Elizabeth I 13
Elphin, diocese of 86, 121, 122
Emly, diocese of 53, 65, 75
English colleges: Lisbon (Sts Peter & Paul) 75, 91, 93, 98, 122, 127–8, 131; Valladolid 16n, 131

[144]

INDEX

Ennis, Edmund 44
Escadinhas de São Crispim 22
Estoril 138
Eudes, blessed John 109n
Eustace, Thomas 113
Everard, James 44, 55
Everard, Sir John 44, 72
Évora, university of 43, 44, 44n, 46, 50, 51, 52, 53, 60, 61, 63, 65, 66, 67, 70, 73, 75, 79, 84, 88, 89, 92, 95, 97, 98, 99, 102, 105, 113
exclaustração 22, 22n

'The Factory' 101
Fallon, James 52
famine in Ireland 132
Fenning, Hugh OP 20, 21
Fernandes Ximenes, António 24, 28, 29, 31, 32, 45, 112
Fernandes de Almada, Luís 30, 59, 107, 108
Ferns 88, 92, 93, 95, 97, 123
Fethard 42, 44, 71, 87
Fielding, Henry 115
Finegan, Francis 20
Fitzgerald, Augustine 43
Fitzgerald, Lord Edward 122
Fitzgerald, James 136
Fitzgerald, Lord Robert 137
Fitzgerald, Thomas 26
Fitzgibbon family 138
Fitzgibbon, Maurice 53
Fitzmaurice Fitzgerald: *see* Fitzgerald
Fonseca, Diego de 28
Fonseca, Pedro de SJ 23, 24n.26, 38, 38n
Foundation masses 29–30, 65, 66, 69, 70, 72, 74, 76, 80, 81, 82, 85, 87, 91, 92, 93, 94, 95, 96
Franciscans 14, 62, 66, 69, 70, 71, 78, 81, 84, 88, 95, 98
Frazão, Francisco 28
French, Revolution 15, 116, 131
French, Walter 38, 42
Funchal 43, 99

Galway 23, 60, 68, 70, 81, 88, 95
Garristown 96
Gazeta de Lisboa 120
Gelarte, George SJ 43
Geraldine family 53n
Geraldinus, Geraldino: *see* Fitzgerald
Germany 86
Gibbons, James SJ 113

Gibbons, Laurence 113
Gibbons, Thomas 113
Goa 31, 54n
Godinez: *see* Wadding
Gomez, Isabel 30, 107, 108
Gortmakellis 64
Greames, Michael 109
Gregorian calendar 33n
Guevara, Luís Rodrigues 28

Hay, Patrick O'Connor: *see* O'Connor
Hennessy, Thomas SJ 48, 113–4
Henrique, cardinal and king 23n, 46
Henry VIII 13
Henry the navigator 27
os hibérnicos 22
Higgins, Edward 112–3
Higgins, John SJ 113
Hogan, Dermot 55
Howling, John SJ 23, 24n, 26, 32, 34, 38, 38n
Hungary 81

Irish colleges: Alcalá de Henares 15, 17, 24n; Bordeaux 15, 122; Lille 78, 121; Madrid 95; Nantes 15; Netherlands 15,; Paris 15, 16, 123; Rome 15, 16, 119; Rouen 15; Salamanca 15, 16, 18, 20, 42, 50, 61, 80, 81, 83, 85, 94, 98, 105, 114, 116; Santiago de Compostela 15, 17, 32, 50, 52; Seville 15, 20, 83, 86, 95; Toulouse 15
Irish language 45
Irmandade 25, 25n, 26

James II 64
Jesuits 15, 16, 17; in Ireland 87; students of Lisbon college 58–99; provincial in Portugal 14, 112; general in Rome 45, 45n, 48, 78, 84, 87, 96, 108, 109, 109n, 110–3; suppression in Spain 15, in Portugal 15, 40
Joana de Cruz, sister 30, 108n
João II 27
João VI 118
John of Gaunt 27
José, king 103,
José, prince of Brazil 138
Joyce, Hyacinth 42, 117, 119, 123, 125, 127
Joyce, Patrick 132, 133
Junot, general 117

[145]

Kearns, Nicolas 134–5
Kearney, David 52
Keene, Sir Benjamin 100
Kelly, Edmund SJ 34, 44
Kelly, Oliver 132
Kelly, Patrick 51
Keohane, Daniel 113
Kilboin 94
Kildare, diocese of 45n, 51, 82, 96
Kilfinan 93
Kilkenny 19, 61.94
Kilkerrin 76
Killala 52, 122
Killaloe, diocese of 32, 34, 51, 52, 60, 63, 70, 74, 77, 84, 87, 88, 89, 90
Killinick 93
Killucan 92
Kilmacow 64
Kilmallock 78
Kilmore, diocese of 53, 73, 85, 129, 137
Kinsale 20
Kinsealy 74
Kirwan, Francis 70
Knoles, Anthony 113

Lacy, de, John 26
Lafoës, duke of 89, 124
Latin 17, 139
Leahy, Dr 129
Lee, Charles SJ 53
Lee, John 15
Lega, Cecilia de 30, 107–8
Lencastre, Luis de 27
Lennon, Father Lennon 120
Levin, Thomas OP 103
Leynich, Nicholas SJ 26, 38, 38n, 55
Lille 78
Limerick 23, 59, 63, 69, 80, 84, 93
Linegar, John 50
Lisbon, archbishop of 28, 52
Lisbon Gas Light Co. 138
Lismore 68, 84, 89, 98
Lisward, Edward SJ 19
Lobinstown 92
Lobo, Alvaro 38
Londonderry, Lord 137
Long family 138
Low Countries 80
Lucena, Juan de SJ 26, 38
Lynch family 138
Lynch, Andrew 55
Lynch, Walter 52

MacBrien, Maurice 53
MacCongail, Donald 52
Machra II, Matthew 55
MacDonald, William 20, 42
MacDonagh, Michael OP 53
MacErlean, John 20
MacGauren, Edmund 53
MacGeoghegan, Rochus OP 51
MacMahon, Ross 83
MacManus, Brian 122
Mac Nally, C 121, 123
Madeira 43
Madrid 28
Magalhães, Cosme de 38
Magalhães, Sebastião 112
Magrath, William 34, 38, 39n, 44n, 45
Manique, viscount 86, 125
Mannion, John 125, 128
Maria I, queen 102, 138
Maria II, 'da Glória' 118
Mascarenhas, Nuno SJ 26
Mathews, Andrew 108
Maynooth 41, 42, 131
Meath 60, 79, 85, 96
Meath Street, Dublin 122
Meirenho-Mor, conde de 27
Melho da Silva, Garcia de 24, 26, 27
Melo, Antonio Jorge de 112
memorial of protest (1624) 61, 68, 93
memorial to General in Rome 109n
Mesa de Consciência 41
Mexia, Afonso de SJ 37, 112
Middleton 41
Moraes, Ormizonda 30
Moore, Tom 137
Morrison: see Mannion
Moura, Joao de 45
Moura 90
Moycashel 83
Moylan, Dr 123
Moyvore 71
Mullen, Barnaby 120
Murphy, Edward 93, 109, 112
Murphy, John 51
Murray, Patrick 42, 129

Nagle, William 34n
Nash, Peter (Father Ignatius) 42
Nenagh 64
Netherlands (Spanish) 15 (Irish colleges at Antwerp, Douai, Lille, Louvain, Tournai)

INDEX

Nevin, Thomas 45, 125
New Christians: see *Cristianos novos*
New Ross 60, 84
Noronha, Garcia de 31
Nossa Senhora do Bom Sucesso: see Bom Sucesso

'oath' 69, 78, 94
O'Brien, John 18, 116
O'Connell, Daniel 138
O'Connor Hay, Patrick 125
O'Crean, Andrew OP 52
O'Daly, Dominic (Daniel) OP 22n, 23, 53n
O'Doherty, Denis 20
O'Gallagher, Redmond 52
O'Hart, Eugene OP 52
O'Herlihy, Thomas 52
Old Ross 92
Oliveiria, José de 105
O'Mahony, Cornelio de S Patricio 42, 44, 44n
O'Mulryan: see Ryan
O'Neill, The, present holder of title, Hugo 138
O'Neill, Brian Ballach 138
O'Neill, Carolina 138
O'Neill, Charles 138
ONeill, Conn 137
O'Neill, Hugo 138
O'Neill Jorge 138
O'Neill, José Maria 138
O'Neill, Shane 137
O'Neills of Clanaboy 137–9
Oporto 43, 53, 65, 99
O'Reilly, Hugh 53
Oristown 85
Ossory 26, 34, 52, 59, 64, 65, 70, 74
O'Sullivan Beare, Domhnall 34
O'Sullivan, Paul OP 124
O'Teig, Donal 52
Oxford 16n

Pacheco, Diego 89
Pallas 72
Pallotto, G.B. 62
Paris 16n
Parma, Ranuccio, duke of 23n
Pedro IV 118
patriarcado 7, 21
Pena Fiel. conde de 122
Penal Laws 13, 37, 47
Peninsular war 41, 105, 116

Persons, Robert 16n
Philip II 16, 16n, 23, 23n, 25
Philippa of Lancaster 27
Plunket, George 122, 123
Pombal, marquês de 15, 22n, 40, 51, 102, 105, 138
Ponte Delgada 44n
Power, Mr 19

quinta 28, 41
Quinta das Machadas 138

Raphoe 52
Rebelho, Francisco 28
rectors: see 38–42; Portuguese rectors 39
Red Cow 83
Redmond, Mr 91, 120, 122
Reformation 13
Richmond, Virginia 79
Rinuccini 72
Roche, Cornelius (da Rocha-MacCarrick) 34, 38, 39n, 55, 109
Rochfort. Robert SJ 53
Rodrigues, Brites Roiz 30
Rome 13, 52, 53, 66, 73, 86, 98
Ross: see Cork, Cloyne, Ross
Rossiter, Michael 50
Russell, Patrick 50, 51, 87
Russell, Patrick OP 124, 129
Ryan, Francis Cornelius 34, 34n, 52, 55, 65, 84, 94

Sacred Heart 109n
St Anthony 25
St Brigid 34n, 53
St Catherine, parish of 92, 94
St Elmo's fire 22n
St Isidore 98
St Joseph of Cluny, sisters of 35
St Leger, John SJ 19
St Malo 81
St Olaf, parish of 77
St Omer 138
St Patrick's chapel, Lisbon 107
St Peter, parish of (Drogheda) 97
St Peter, parish of (Waterford) 97
St Paul, parish of 99
St Robert, parish of 97
Salamanca: see Irish colleges
Saldanha, Francisco de 104, 105
Santiago de Compostela 32, 50, 52, 98
Santiago de Compostela: see Irish colleges

São Roque 24, 24n, 28, 34, 52
Scilly 18
Scottish college 16n
Setúbal 138
Seville 83, 86
Seville: see Irish colleges
Shea, Fr SJ 19
Sheepstown 94
Sherlock, Bartholomew 41, 103n, 105
Sherlock, Paul SJ 32
Sherry, William 105
Silke, John J. 20
Skerret, Nicholas 24n, 52
Sleyne, John Baptist 53, 92
Soares, Manuel 111
Sousa, Gaspar de 28
Southey, Robert 115
Stafford, Nicholas 110
Stamullen 69
Stansast, Walter 32
Stonley, Samuel 32
Strabane 82
Strangford, Lord 137
Strong, Thomas 26
Sweetman, Nicholas 40
Swords 96
Syon Abbey 100

Talbot, Patrick SJ 50, 51
Tanner, Edmund 53
Tavares, Francisco 112, 113
Terzo, Filippo 34
Thomastown 69
Torlade & Co 138
Trent, council of 14, 64, 52
Tribunal Administrativo do Circulo de Lisboa 35
Troy, John Thomas OP 40, 46, 78, 86, 88, 91, 103, 105, 118, 120, 121, 123, 124, 125
Tuam 18, 51, 52, 61, 78, 81, 121
Tyrawley, Lord 137

Urban VIII 37

Valladolid 16, 60, 62, 76, 98
Varatejo 107
Verdon, John 37
Verdon, John, bishop of Ferns 50
Vianna, João António 125
viaticum 17, 18, 80
Vieira Senior, António 31
Vila Verde, count of 120

Wadding, Luke OFM 45, 52, 65, 71
Wadding, Luke 50
Wadding, Matthew 53n
Wale, Patrick FitzRichard 98
Wall, Patrick 55
Walsh, Thomas 51
Walsh, William 24n
Waterford 18, 19, 23, 43, 51, 60, 64, 65, 71, 77, 80, 91, 97, 99
Wellesley, Arthur, duke of Wellington 117, 137
Westmeath 64
Westport 132
Wexford 88, 93
White, Francis 55
White Matthew 43
White, Michael SJ 18
White Stephen 55
White, Thomas SJ 15, 16, 32, 34, 38, 38n, 45
Williams, Mrs 137
Witham, Kitty 100
Wolfe, David SJ 53

Xabregas 62
Ximenes de Aragão, Jerónimo 29, 30, 66
Ximenes, Tomás 29

Yate, Joannes 32n

BX 920 .L55 O26 2001
O'Connell, Patricia.
The Irish College at Lisbon,
1590-1834